The Cat, the Rat, & Lovell the Dog

Susan Collingbourne

Copyright © 2023

All Rights Reserved

To my husband Andrew for his unflagging enthusiasm and encouragement.

Acknowledgments

Mr. Kenneth Williams, for the time he gave me during my visit to Cambridge. I am indebted to him for sharing his research material and for guiding me to the Patent Rolls, Close Rolls and Fine Rolls and other resources in various libraries in England.

Thank you to the Richard III Society for allowing me to participate in The Triennial Conference at Cambridge University, April 2005. I must express my gratitude to the speakers who talked to me later about my research and gave suggestions for further possibilities.

Table of Contents

Prologue ix
Chapter 1 1
Chapter 2 6
Chapter 3 19
Chapter 4 34
Chapter 5 42
Chapter 6 51
Chapter 7 64
Chapter 8 72
Chapter 9 86
Chapter 10 97
Chapter 11 110
Chapter 12 124
Chapter 13 131
Chapter 14 136
Chapter 15 149
Chapter 16 163
Chapter 17 176
Chapter 18 196
Chapter 19 210
Chapter 20 221
Chapter 21 233
Chapter 22 250
Chapter 23 261
Afterword 273

Prologue

One night in July 1484, just a year into the reign of Richard III, a man walked to St. Paul's Cathedral in London. He was not young. If the light was better, one would see tinges of grey in his hair and even a sign of balding. He walked with a good gait, standing tall. There was an air of dignity about him that suggested he was well-bred. His clothes, too, were made of quality cloth, far too superior to the coarse fabric worn by peasants. When he reached the doors of the cathedral, he looked about him. There was not a soul in sight. He slowly withdrew a roll of parchment from under his cloak. Carefully he unrolled the sheet and affixed doggerel to the great doors of St. Paul's. He stood back and slowly read out the words:

The Cat, the Rat, and Lovell the dog
Rule all England under the hog.

He let out a soft, disdainful chuckle. Turned and walked away without a backward glance.

It was not clear who first discovered the lampoon and a mystery who would have dared to write it, but within days King Richard had been informed. He stared at his informant, a miserable-looking man whose trembling hands held the message torn from the massive cathedral door. Richard's men had drawn lots to determine who would be bold enough to present the rhyme to the king. The unfortunate man who had drawn the short straw watched the king as he read the offensive words and waited for the king's response. Richard recognised the allegory was an insult to himself and his three closest supporters. He looked up at the man, still trembling, his enlarged thyroid wobbling with each gulp. Although slightly irritated to see his fear, Richard spoke kindly. "Do we know who is responsible for this?" The man shook his head, clearly relieved the king showed no apparent anger. Richard shrugged his shoulders. "I've more pressing concerns." He handed the scrappy piece of parchment back to the messenger and left the room.

A glorious day some weeks later, William Collingbourne was in his gardens at Lydiad throwing a ball for his dog Roary. The beautiful brown water spaniel chased the ball, his ears bobbing as he loped across the lawn. Sir Walter Hungerford stood beside Collingbourne, watching Roary retrieving. He was a tall, thin-faced man with dark wavy hair. His long legs showed off dark blue tights. Fur trimmed a lighter blue tunic. There was something in his manner that suggested wealth and breeding. His lined face looked friendly but grave. Suddenly he spoke. "Richard has offered a reward for information regarding that seditious verse nailed to the doors of St. Paul's." Collingbourne looked at Hungerford and then roared with laughter. He picked up the ball, dropped at his feet, and threw it hard. Roary leapt after it. Sir Walter eyed Collingbourne suspiciously. "What do you know about it, William?" Collingbourne, watching Roary, began to recite.

> *The crookbackt Boar the way hath found*
> *To root our Roses from our ground*
> *Both flower and bud he hath confound*
> *The King of Beasts, the swine, is crown'd*
> *And now the Dog, the Cat, and Rat*
> *Shall in his trough feed and be fat.*

Walter shook his head, smiling. "You'll go too far one of these days, William. What does it mean anyway?" Roary dropped the ball and began nudging Collingbourne to throw it again. He picked it up and pretended to throw it but hid it behind his back. Roary watched him carefully. He wasn't fooled.

"They're all out for what they can get," Collingbourne spoke bitterly as he threw the ball even harder. Sir Walter, his voice almost inaudible, said, "You, of all men, should know what caution is. Richard will show you no mercy if he finds you out. They watched the dog loping back and drop the ball at Sir Walter's feet. He picked it up and passed it to Collingbourne. It flew high in the air. Roary sprung like a puppy and pounced on the ball as it bounced.

"The man's a swine." Collingbourne's sudden outburst caused Roary to race over in alarm. He sat and looked up at his master, head on one side. William bent and stroked his ears. "All the years we worked side by side. Richard was so loyal to his brother, the king. I believed in them. I was fooled then, but no more! No more! He will pay the price. I'll see that he does."

Sir Walter, startled by his anger, lay a hand on his friend's shoulder. "Such rage William. If your anger is against Richard, no good will come of it. You have always been so supportive of the Yorkists. Edward was your friend. What or who has changed you?"

Chapter 1

Early April 1461. On the grounds of Windsor Castle, under the shade of huge Oak trees, a rowdy group of young men lolled around, swigging their ale. Loud bursts of raucous laughter drew the attention of passers-by. They were obviously very drunk and had good reason to celebrate, for they were victors of the Battle of Towton. Edward IV of York, a young man of only eighteen, had deposed the Lancastrian Henry VI and secured the English throne. The young king was enjoying himself with friends and followers.

Tall and proud, he stood up rather unsteady on his feet and waved his goblet to his men. "I say it was the bloodiest victory ever won on English soil!" He looked around at his men, who grunted and cheered in agreement.

"We sent Margaret and her slave scurrying to Scotland with that son of theirs," called a man with hair the colour of carrots. His voice was loud, and he punctuated his comment with a tremendous burp. The men clapped in approval. There was little respect for King Henry.

Collingbourne, who had been sitting next to the king, stood up and waved his goblet. Although he was tall and well-built, the king looked down at him. "Your father would be proud of you." Collingbourne's speech was slurred. The king put an arm around his friends' shoulders. "Ludgershall for you. Yes, I've decided to grant you the office of keeper of my park of Ludgershall. Be loyal to me, Collingbourne, and you'll not regret it." Edward gave him a hearty slap on the back.

Collingbourne, although pleased, was distracted by a young lady who curtsied to the king as she passed. Edward gave a loud roar of laughter. 'You have an eye for the ladies, I see. Too bad that one is taken."

"Who is she?" Collingbourne asked, his eyes fixed on her. Edward laughed again. "Margaret, Countess of Richmond. Henry Stafford has just married that pretty lass. I can't help you there. I'm keeping my eye on her, though. She comes from a very bothersome Lancastrian family."

Collingbourne stared after her. Her pale blue gown moved with the sway of her slim body. Hair cascaded over her shoulders, held in place by her headdress. He watched as she approached the castle and, giving a quick glance over her shoulder and a shy smile, passed through the arch.

Edward leaned closer to Collingbourne and whispered into his ear. I met the most beautiful woman the other day. Collingbourne looked interested. He knew Edward had an eye for a pretty lass. He raised his eyebrows, smiled, and said softly, "Tell me more." The king did not elaborate but turned away. It was too personal. How surprised he had been when he received a letter asking for an audience from Lady Eleanor, who had become the widow of Sir Thomas Butler, a Lancastrian supporter. Edward recalled he had seized both her properties because her father-in-law had not completed the paperwork obtaining a licence for the transfer of title. He remembered the scene clearly. He was more interested in her than the properties and was acutely embarrassed when she began crying. He had taken her hands in his own and spoken tenderly. "You must understand that Lord Sudeley was wrong to convey the manors to you and your husband without a royal licence." She lowered her head, trying to hide her tears. Lifting her chin with a finger and observing how distressed she was, he weakened. He spoke gently as he brushed aside a tear. "I will pardon him and return your manors." Then with a change of tone, "now, surely you will allow me to dine with you?" He was confident the relationship would flower. What he hadn't expected was a refusal of his advances. She had denied him despite his argument that he had promised to return her properties or that he was the king and she, his subject. She had responded rather curtly that a king should know better than ask a lady of noble birth to become his mistress. Although it irritated him, it made her more desirable. He clenched his fists. Damn Warwick and his interference. Damn the French alliance. He would choose his own bride.

Collingbourne noted the way Edward suddenly clenched his fists and then began to click his fingers – a sign he was agitated. It wasn't wise to comment.

The sun had begun to glow red and disappear behind the castle. Edward threw his goblet on the table and beckoned his companions to hasten inside. A banquet had been prepared, and he, for one, was hungry. They would all meet within the great hall when the clock struck eight. He gave a sidelong look at Collingbourne, "Your lady friend will be there; a shame her husband will be too." Laughing, he strode off towards the castle.

Later at the banquet, Edward took the opportunity to introduce Collingbourne to Margaret, Countess of Richmond. Collingbourne was struck by the direct gaze of her grey eyes. She smiled warmly. He felt an immediate connection. Edward, amused, winked at William and whisked Henry Stafford away to meet Lord Henry Higginbottom. He was sure that Stafford would be very interested in his lordship, who seemed, like Midas, to have the ability to turn everything to gold.

Margaret, too was amused. She was well aware of the king's interest in romance and quite happy to play his games. William's words made her start.

"I am amazed you are at court with Edward when your family has been so opposed to him." She was not expecting such a blunt comment, but undeterred, she replied, "I need to keep in favour with the King, if only for my son."

"Ah, yes, your son. Where is he?"

"He lives with his uncle in Wales. I have every faith that Jasper will protect him. Certainly, he is safer there than here with me." William noticed the challenge in her grey eyes. He knew Edward didn't trust her. Her son was a nephew of King Henry and a contender to the throne in the eyes of Lancastrians. There would be many who wanted him out of the way. She had good reason to be concerned.

"It must be very difficult for you." His unexpected empathetic words brought unwanted tears. Without thinking, William took her hand and gently patted it. He had the urge to take her in his arms and comfort her, to take away the pain. She smiled, leaving her hand longer in his than she should have before she withdrew. It was a memory he had treasured for years. Whether she knew it or not, she had captured his heart.

Chapter 2

A young girl of thirteen stood in a beautiful blue gown of velvet in which she had been dressed. She placed her hand against the skirt, enjoying the softness of the fabric. Her eyes rested on the sleeves that widened just before the wrist and were studded with pearls. She gave a delighted sigh, for she had never had a dress so magnificent that made her feel so grown up. Eleanor Talbot, still only a child, was about to become the wife of Thomas Boutler, the only son of Lord Sudeley. Today, she had her very own servant girls who were preparing her for her wedding. Her hair, brushed for well over the hundred strokes normally applied before bedtime, hung like black silk, the light catching the sheen as she moved. Her dresser added just a small headdress, also studded with pearls.

Eleanor lifted one foot to admire the attractive blue satin shoes, pleased with how closely they matched the colour of her dress.

Margaret Beauchamp, Countess of Shrewsbury, hurried into the room. She stopped short when her daughter faced her. Still a child but already evidence of the beautiful woman she was to become. She smiled. "How grown up you look. Quite lovely. Eleanor flushed with pleasure and curtseyed to her mother, who, although proud, felt a moment's sadness that her little daughter had grown up and was leaving home. She smiled and held out her hand. "Come, my dear; they are all waiting in the chapel."

Eleanor had never met her prospective husband. She had only seen Lord Sudeley and Lady Sudeley once on their visit to meet their future daughter-in-law. They had both been very kind. She liked them very much. Her young sister, Elizabeth, when hearing Eleanor would live in a castle, laughed and said she would be a princess.

Indeed Eleanor felt like a princess as heads turned to watch her walking to join Thomas Sudeley, who was waiting with the Bishop. She thought he was quite handsome but very old. Although he smiled, she could sense he was nervous. She wondered what there was to be nervous about. Perhaps he thought he would not remember what to say. Eleanor was confident. She had been informed what the Bishop would say and how she should answer. She had learnt her lines well.

Later, when they sat at the long table to enjoy the celebratory banquet, her new husband had whispered she should not worry if he seemed old because she would soon catch up with him and become a lady. Eleanor blushed and wondered if he could read her mind. She was not really worried because her mother had emphasised how lucky she was to be marrying Thomas. His father was an earl, and one day Thomas would be an earl. Her mother had told her that after the marriage, she would live with her father-in-law Lord Sudeley and his wife in Sudeley Castle. No one had explained that her marriage would not be consummated until she was older. There was plenty of time for Eleanor to learn what was expected of a good wife.

Eleanor enjoyed living with her new family. She didn't see much of Thomas because he was mostly away fighting for the Lancastrian cause. The family talked a lot about the Lancastrians. It was rather confusing because although King Henry was King, some said he went mad and couldn't be king anymore. Then he got well again, and all was well. His wife was French, but some people didn't like her very much. She had asked her mother once, were French people horrible. Her mother had been cross and said it was a silly question.

Eleanor was kept busy learning what it meant to be a wife and mother. She also learned some history about her father-in-law. She learned that he had been a brilliant politician and became Lord

Chamberlain of King Henry's household, and the following year he became Treasurer of the King's Exchequer. She hadn't really understood what it meant, but she imagined he was in charge of a huge treasure.

In 1452 Lord Sudeley transferred three manors to his son. Eleanor was told it was time their marriage was consummated. She would move to Fenny Compton with her husband, who didn't seem quite as old now. There she was mistress of the manor and would put into practice all the things she had learned.

The housekeeper, who was much older than Eleanor, helped her young mistress with decisions she wasn't sure about. It didn't take long for Eleanor to feel confident. She was happy. She loved Fenny Compton, which was now her home, particularly the gardens where she enjoyed long walks through the beautiful forests. Thomas was kind and patient. She was aware that as the months passed by, Thomas hoped for the news that an heir was on the way. She prayed they would soon be blessed with a child.

Months passed to years. Her mother-in-law, Lady Sudeley, asked her once if everything was as it should be in her married life. She had blushed profusely and had assured her that it was. Lady Sudeley took her hand. "Don't worry, my dear; it will happen at the right time. God is good, and you are still very young." Eleanor wondered if Lord Sudeley had spoken to Thomas about the matter. Thomas had not said anything to her.

Her sister Elizabeth often came to stay, particularly when Thomas was away. Soon her sister would be married to Henry, the Duke of Norfolk. It was to be a grand affair, and she, too, would live in a castle. "Not as a princess, Eleanor teased, but as a duchess." She wondered how long it would take for her sister to conceive a child.

Three years had passed since Eleanor had moved to Fenny Compton as mistress of her own manor when in May 1455, Lord Sudeley had rushed to find his wife, who was quietly engaged in her embroidery. She saw immediately by his red face and breathlessness that something was wrong. "The king has called us to arms! I must go, my love. The Duke of Somerset is in trouble at St. Albans." Already men had gathered, and the noise of horses whinnying and men shouting could be heard.

"Thomas, is Thomas to go with you?" Lady Sudely had thrust her needlework aside and followed her husband as he left the room.

He turned, gathered her in his arms, holding her so tightly she could hardly breath. "I have no doubt Thomas has already gone. Goodbye, my sweeting. We will crush those who threaten our king. Take care 'til I return." He gave her a kiss and was gone.

When Eleanor received the parchment with her father-in-law's seal, she trembled. She tore the seal and read the message. "My dear daughter, Our king is in danger. I must respond to the call to arms. I understand this is a very worrying time for you and my dear wife. Perhaps you could stay with her until I return."

Eleanor felt suddenly cold. War! Of course, she would go immediately to her mother-in-law. She called her servants to prepare for the journey as quickly as possible. Within an hour, they were ready. It did not take long. She sent a prayer to heaven. "Please keep them safe. And King Henry, keep him safe too."

Lady Sudeley was pleased to see her daughter-in-law. "Such terrible news." They settled in comfortable chairs in Lady Sudeley's private room. It was smaller than the other rooms in the castle. The prospect faced northeast, and the sun shone through the tall gothic windows for most of the year. White-washed walls gave the room light. Magnificent tapestries and huge luxurious rugs created a comfortable atmosphere. The room was well-lit at night by very large candles fitted in marble stands. In winter, a huge fire could be heard crepitating, and heat permeated every corner of the room. This day in May had begun with beautiful sunshine, welcome after the fickle month of April, but dark clouds were gathering on the horizon. Lady Sudeley frowned. A bad omen, but not wishing to worry Eleanor, she said nothing.

"This trouble has been brewing for a long time," Lady Sudeley remarked as she threaded wool through her needle. They had enjoyed a simple meal of meats and fruit. Despite the sunshine during the day, the late afternoon was chilly. Lady Sudeley had instructed a fire be lit to cheer everything up.

Eleanor nodded. "The problem is Richard, the Duke of Richmond, thinks he has a better entitlement to the throne than King Henry, particularly since he was recalled to court as Henry's closest adult relative."

Lady Sudeley lowered her voice. "It doesn't help with that French queen of his. She is not liked at all. No wonder King Henry has his little turns." Eleanor shivered. She had heard that some of his courtiers said he was mad. Was it treason to say such a thing? But it was true. The Duke of York had been made Lord Protector and ruled while Henry suffered his complete breakdown. The thing was, Henry recovered.

There was a crash of thunder. The room began to get ominously darkened. Lady Sudeley called for a servant to attend to the huge drapes and light the candles.

It was not until Lord Sudeley returned a few days later that his wife and daughter-in-law learned the bitter outcome. They had lost. The Duke of Buckingham had arrived with 2000 men, and he, not Somerset, was in command.

Lord Sudeley mumbled angrily. "Somerset made a right stuff up! The king lost faith in him. We didn't stand a chance. Yorkists had over 4000 men to our 2000. We were hopelessly outnumbered."

He sighed as he sunk into a chair and accepted a mug of ale. "York tried to negotiate." His voice was flat. "We were mighty glad about that. We had no chance with those numbers against us. But they wanted Somerset's blood, and the king wouldn't agree. His words were strong."

Eleanor leaned forward. 'What happened? How did you lose?"

Lord Sudeley took a gulp of his ale. "I think the Duke lost patience. The next thing we knew, they were upon us. They had decided to attack. Somerset had sought refuge in Castle Inn, then, like a mad man; he came charging out, killing anyone in his way until he was struck down. There were arrows flying from every direction, striking those guarding the king. Even the king was injured – and Buckingham. We had no archers to retaliate. I saw immediately we were outflanked. Our men ran for their lives. We didn't have a chance." His voice expressed the despair they felt.

Lady Sudeley whispered the question. "They have the king?" Her voice rose. "They let them take King Henry? Shame on them!" She looked in disgust at her husband.

Eleanor put an arm around her. "They didn't really have a choice, mother. The king will be safe. It was better than more men losing their lives. We must pray for their souls." She turned to her father-in-law. "What about Thomas? Did you see Thomas?" He shook his head. "Many of the men were not involved. Sweet Jesus, let us pray Thomas was among them."

Thomas arrived at Fenny Compton the following day. Eleanor hurried home and was there to greet him. She ran to him. He held her in his arms, kissing her gently. She traced a finger around his tired face. "Have you heard how fares the king?"

"Warwick and the Duke of York have escorted him to London. I expect he is in The Tower by now. Buckingham is dead, and Queen Margaret has fled into exile, taking her young son with her. The Duke of York is appointed the Protector of England." Eleanor saw the worried lines on his brow. "It will not be the end of it," he sighed wearily as, with his arm around Eleanor, they walked through the archway of the entrance to Fenny Compton. "Margaret will be back with another army, and there will be more bloodshed. Happy that Thomas had returned safely, they made love. Eleanor listened while Thomas slept. She made a silent prayer that this time God would bless them and she could present her husband with a son. However, God could not have been listening because, in a few weeks, it had become evident she had failed to conceive. Thomas found her crying. She knew Thomas was disappointed, but he placed no blame on her. "We must be patient. God will send us a child when the time is right." Eleanor felt anger. She had been told so many times the time had to be right, but when would that be?

Thomas was right. The Lancastrian queen had threatened to return. Thomas once more put on his armour and answered the call to arms.

Eleanor was sewing when Lord Sudeley unexpectedly arrived, his face haggard and grey. He stood and stared at Eleanor, his bottom lip trembling. Eleanor didn't need to hear the words. It was Thomas – he was dead. He was one of the 2000 Lancastrian men killed at the Battle of Blore Heath on 23rd September.

Eleanor felt numb. Why did men continue to fight each other? So many mothers cried for the loss of their sons, wives grieved for their menfolk, and children left without a father. It was all so futile! The fight for the possession of a crown.

Thomas Lord Sudeley's only child was gone. She had failed to give him an heir. It had been seven years of married life. Perhaps if Thomas had not always been off fighting wars... She was only 23. There would have been time. She looked at her father-in-law, now hunched, as he sunk into a chair. All his dynastic ambitions had crumbled. He was a broken man. Putting her sewing aside, Eleanor went to him, knelt, and took his hands. "Father, I will go home with you. This is not a time to be alone. We can mourn Thomas together."

Months passed, and Eleanor watched as both Lord and Lady Sudeley lost weight and sat most of the day looking blank - lost in memories. One day, Lord Sudeley entered the room with a quickened step.

"I have something to show you." He unrolled a huge sheet of parchment on the table. "Come, look." He spoke excitedly. There spread out before them was a plan of a beautiful church.

"It's to be St. Mary's." A smile deepened the lines on his face. "A fine memorial for Thomas, don't you think?" The smile faded. "See the Gothic windows and the tower. It is to be built in red stone." He stared down at the drawing.

"What a wonderful idea," Eleanor spoke with enthusiasm. He looked at his wife for approval. She wiped away a tear. 'I think so, too."

"I have another surprise for you, Eleanor, my dear." Lord Sudeley rolled up the plans. He picked up another document. "This confirms a quitclaim to you in respect of Fenny Compton. From its date 15th January, I have resigned all title to Fenny Compton to you. The property is now in your own right, not in dower." Once again, a smile, although his eyes looked sad. Eleanor was surprised. How generous of her father-in-law. He just patted her on her shoulder and turned to his wife. "For you, my darling, I have traded a bit of landed property we don't need for prayers for our souls, including Thomas." He bent to kiss her cheek. Neither knew how soon those prayers would be heard.

Lady Eleanor had hardly overcome the shock of her husband's death on the battlefield of Blore Heath when she received another. The letter with the Royal Seal of King Edward IV read:

You are informed that King Edward IV has confiscated the Manors of Burton Dassett and Fenny Compton, previously the properties of your late husband, Sir Thomas Boetler.

What did it mean? Why would the new king confiscate her properties?

When she handed the letter to Lord Sudeley, his face became almost purple with rage. Worde exploded from him. "The young upstart, a Yorkist, who has stolen the crown from the rightful King Henry, has the audacity to seize my family property as well. "Why I'll...I'll..." He didn't finish. Breathless, he collapsed into a nearby chair. Lady Sudeley hurried to him, offering water.

"My Lord, take care, take care. You will do yourself harm. Isn't it bad enough I have lost my son? I cannot lose you too." He clutched her arm, weeping.

Eleanor left the room, Lady Sudeley's voice comforting her husband. She would write to the king and ask for an audience. Surely this matter could be sorted.

A short reply noted that King Edward was not available as he was engaged in matters of his kingdom. Infuriated, she wrote again, mentioning that she came from a noble family and had requested an audience to understand why he had seized her property.

The king agreed to visit her at Fenny Compton. He said he would be in the area the following week. Irritated, she mumbled he probably wanted to inspect his newly acquired manor. She told no one of his impending visit.

Chapter 3

Eleanor, watching from the window, was surprised to see a very tall, strapping young man, elegantly dressed, and walking alone through the gardens. She had never met Edward of York, but she had no doubt this man was the young king. Slightly nervous, she made her way to meet him. She had heard he was a handsome man but had not expected to be quite as impressed. He smiled. "I left my horse at the gate," She curtsied, annoyed to find him so attractive. This was not a good start. She had wondered whether she should act the helpless widow or whether to take a stand. He looked around and spotted the bench under the old oak tree. "No need for formalities; may I suggest we sit on that bench there under the tree and discuss why you have requested an audience." She acquiesced, and they sat, looking at each other in silence. She thought how incongruous it was, seated on a garden bench with the King of England. They were strangers, sitting together as if they had known each other for years. He said nothing, but she detected a look of amusement in his eye. She bristled. This was not an amusing matter. Frustrated by anger, she burst into tears. He looked alarmed. Edward was never a man to cope with a woman in tears. He leaned forward, concerned. Angry with herself, she blurted, "I am wondering why you, a man of such wealth, would confiscate a widow's property for no apparent reason." He flushed. He had looked into the matter.

"You must understand that Lord Sudeley was wrong to convey the manors to you and your husband without royal licence." Eleanor sighed. She had no idea why her father-in-law had not applied for a royal licence to transfer his properties. Perhaps it was just unfortunate that Henry was no longer king. Was the Yorkist king punishing Lord Sudeley for his sympathy to the House of Lancaster? She didn't know. She had to admit Lord Sudeley had made an error of judgment.

"I do understand Lord Sudeley was wrong." Her words were almost inaudible. "But isn't it enough my husband died fighting a war for the throne of England? You leave me homeless, your majesty." She fought back the tears. Edward could be a harsh man when it suited him, but watching this beautiful young woman struggling to control emotions aroused pity. The manors were not really of interest to him. It was true his motivation in seizing them was to punish Lord Sudeley. He was far more interested in developing a relationship with Eleanor.

He took her hand and said graciously, "I will pardon him and return your manors." He stood. I must leave you now but will return tomorrow if you would honour me with your company. It would give me such pleasure to take a walk through that magnificent Beech forest you have.

Eleanor was sorry he was going so soon. She hadn't offered him refreshments. He must think her so rude, but it hadn't been her intention to make him welcome.

When Lady Elizabeth Talbot visited her sister, she was delighted to see that Eleanor had cast off the miserable gloom of late.

"It is good to see you happy again, Eleanor." Surprised to see her sister blush, she pressed her for news. Eleanor confided that King Edward had promised to pardon Lord Sudeley and return her properties.

"He really is a very attractive man. You will like him."

Elizabeth was surprised. "I will like him? Does he visit? Eleanor blushed again and gave a shy smile. "Yes. He comes quite often. We take walks together in the forests, and last week he brought a horse, and we spent a day together.

Elizabeth's face crumpled in concern. "Oh, Eleanor. He has a reputation. Young women are not safe with him. You must be careful. He is very powerful, and I have heard he is charming, but he could crush you like a bird if he had a mind to."

"But why should he, Elizabeth? We love each other. I have never known such love. Thomas was more an older brother than a lover. I am so very, very happy." Elizabeth felt a sense of misgiving but simply replied. "You are too trusting, sister dear. Are you his mistress? Once he has had his pleasure, he will drop you without a thought."

"Shame on you, Elizabeth. I am of noble birth. I will not become the mistress of any man." She was hurt. Her sister should think so little of her. She thrust out her chin in defiance. "He is a man of honour and respects me."

Elizabeth gave a cynical laugh. "If you are thinking he will marry you, forget it. They will never allow it. I heard there are arrangements for a French princess to be his bride."

Eleanor laughed. "He knows that but says it will never happen."

"Do you think he will have a choice?" Elizabeth scoffed. She leaned forward and wrapped her arms around her sister. Her voice softened. "Do be careful, be happy, but very careful."

"I am Elizabeth. I am very happy. Please do not tell anyone, though. It is our secret. You are the only person I have told. Edward says it will be time to tell the world when we are ready.

Elizabeth promised. She was pleased to see her sister happy and in love, but she wished it was not with the king. She thought about her own wedding planned for October. She would become the Duchess of Norfolk. She liked the Duke, it was an advantageous marriage, but she didn't have the shine in her eyes that Eleanor had when she spoke of Edward.

Lord Sudeley was surprised his daughter-in-law had been honoured to receive a request to attend King Edward's coronation, but then she had astonished him more when she told him the king had agreed to return her properties. The command to attend the coronation himself angered him. Why would he want to participate in the coronation of a Yorkist king? It was insulting. His loyalty was to King Henry, the rightful king, not to this usurper. He waved the document in Eleanor's face. "First, the king returns your property, and now this? What is going on, Eleanor? God's oath, you need to take care. He loves a dalliance with a pretty woman."

Lady Sudeley attempted to calm him. "My lord, you can hardly blame Eleanor because our new king asks for your loyalty and support. It will do us no service to offend him. You should do as Eleanor does. Flatter him, or at least don't offend him. To do otherwise is foolish." Her husband grumbled under his breath. "I'll go. Of course, I will. I don't have much choice, but I'd far rather Henry wasn't pushed off his throne by that usurper." His wife hushed him. His words were dangerous. It wouldn't do if they were conveyed to King Edward.

Edward IV was crowned on 28th June 1461. It was a spectacular occasion. Eleanor, together with her sister Elizabeth, was placed in seats close to the king. If anyone had objections, they hadn't been voiced. She was proud of Edward. He looked so dignified, so regal, and he was hers.

She tried to concentrate, but other images crept into her vision. Walking through forests, holding his hand; racing on horseback to avoid the storm; her headdress dislodged, flying off in the wind. How they had laughed. There was a loud crash, and the heavens opened. Cuddling together under a huge tree, rain droplets from her drenched hair trickling down her face. He licked them off, whispering "delicious" as he tasted the salt. He kissed her and whispered, "I can't wait to make you mine, my darling. Shall I ask Stillington to meet us in your chapel, and we will be married?"

Loud music interrupted her thoughts. She recalled where she was. Her sister Elizabeth whispered, "You should be there with him." Eleanor gave her a gentle kick.

Eleanor sat in her private chambers in Framlingham Castle, the home of her sister Elizabeth, Duchess of Norfolk. Lord Sudeley had lost his wife of forty years not long after the death of his son.

He became very lonely. In just over a year, he had remarried. His wife, Alice Deincourt, was the grandmother of Francis, Viscount Lovell. Clearly, the marriage was not in the hope of an heir, as she was about sixty years old. Eleanor was pleased for him. She was free to spend more time with her sister Elizabeth.

Eleanor and her sister were very close, and Elizabeth had insisted that Eleanor have rooms of her own for her frequent visits. The room was large and, like every room in the castle, walls decorated by magnificent tapestries. There were glazed windows and tiled floors. A huge fireplace, guarded by fire dogs, made the room very comfortable in the colder months.

Eleanor gazed out of the windows at the beauty of the gardens. It had been two years since she and Edward had secretly married in the chapel at Fenny Compton. Eleanor had insisted there be a priest, although Edward would not permit other witnesses. He said he wanted no interference. He had allowed, rather reluctantly, her sister Elizabeth to join their celebration dinner, providing she promised to keep the secret until he had informed Warwick. Elizabeth was hesitant. She was not sure that she really trusted Edward, but for her sister's sake, she joined them.

Edward had been very loving and generous, but his constant need to attend affairs of state and even go to battle meant their time together was not as often as when they enjoyed the first flush of their love. Edward had given her a Wiltshire property that comprised the manor of Oare-under-Savernake., but she had noticed a cooling in their relationship. Edward had not made public their marriage, and if she mentioned it, he changed the subject. Perhaps her sister had been right. He couldn't be trusted.

A few months ago, her sister had announced that Edward was having a very close relationship with Henry, Duke of Somerset. So intimate that he sometimes shared his bedroom. Edward denied it was serious, arguing his intention was to win over Henry, a Lancastrian, to be loyal to him, a Yorkist King. Somerset was influential in the Lancastrian court. Eleanor was persuaded it was just a matter of politics. This had been confirmed in her mind when she learned that Somerset, knowing well that King Henry did not have the strength to oppose the power of King Edward, who had done him great honour, had still supported Henry. Away from Edward's court, fellow Lancastrians had persuaded Somerset that he owed his allegiance and loyalty to King Henry, Margaret of Anjou, and the men with whom he had fought. Somerset, motivated by honour, betrayed King Edward, his friend. Eleanor had hoped Edward would return to her. He did for a few weeks just after she had returned to Fenny Compton. He had been very loving, and their relationship was reminiscent of earlier days of their marriage. Eleanor was sure it would not be long before Edward told Warwick their secret. Weeks passed, but the king made no contact with her. She knew he had been involved in a conspiracy by the Lancastrians. She felt sick with worry. She missed him so much. Depression began to take hold of her. At first, there were tears, then anger bubbled up, so unexpectantly and so forceful it frightened her. It was time Edward announced his marriage. She chastised herself for allowing him to treat her this way. She would write to him and give an ultimatum. She decided to return to Framlington Castle.

That night, the Duke of Norfolk returned from court. They had hardly sat down for dinner when he told them of the shocking news King Edward had delivered to Warwick. The king was secretly married. He had been for several months. He looked around the table to see how the news had been received. Elizabeth shot a look at Eleanor, who was blushing profusely. Had Edward acknowledged their marriage at last?

"Did he give her name?" Eleanor spoke quietly. Didn't her brother-in-law realise it was she who was married to King Edward?

"Oh yes. Elizabeth Woodville. The daughter of Jacquetta of Luxembourg, Dowager Duchess of Bedford. Warwick is furious. Edward has made him look a fool. He had the marriage to the French Princess settled. What an insult it will be to tell her she is not wanted." He sounded amused. Eleanor said no more. She had lost her appetite and excused herself from the table. When she had left the room, the Duke commented that he hadn't expected her to take the news so badly but shrugged his shoulders. "By the devil's tongue, I'll never understand women." Elizabeth said nothing.

"You must challenge him, Eleanor. You have a witness - call the priest. I can speak up too." It was the following morning, and the sisters were taking a walk in the gardens. Eleanor sensed the danger and futility of making such a claim and simply shook her head.

Elizabeth lost patience. "For God's sake, Eleanor, he has betrayed you. Your marriage is lawful. Why won't you defend yourself? You are the legal Queen of England. Stand up for your rights. You must." Eleanor bit her lip and tried to hold back the tears. She wanted to tell her sister that she knew in her heart it was impossible. She was useless to him. For over a year, they had loved each other, but there was no child. How disappointed she was when there was no child when she was married to Thomas. She thought and hoped it might have been Thomas' fault. Now she realised that was not the case. She understood Edward needed an heir. She didn't explain to Elizabeth how she felt, just infuriated her by shaking her head again.

"So, you will allow Edward to cast you aside and not acknowledge you are his wife? Her sister had sounded disappointed but said no more. Eleanor decided to go back to her home if only to escape her sister's looks of despair.

Queen Elizabeth was crowned in May of the following year.

Eleanor's marriage appeared forgotten. However, it was not. Edward spent sleepless nights worried that Eleanor would claim her rights. He had loved her; he couldn't deny that. But his first duty was to have an heir. He had been generous. He had transferred the Manor of Oare-under-Savernake months before his marriage to Elizabeth Woodville. Elizabeth! Such a beauty; she was a widow who had two sons. She had proved she could give him a son. As for Eleanor, well, she would be fine. She was young. Perhaps he could find a husband for her. The Wiltshire property included 'lands, tenements, rents, reversions and services' in Draycote, Coldcot. Eleanor had an income; that should keep her quiet. Nevertheless, thoughts kept creeping into his mind. She might talk. His marriage to Elizabeth was not secure.

Eleanor had remained silent. However, the truth has a way of presenting itself. Queen Elizabeth was surprised to receive a note from someone pertaining to know of a secret that would prove her marriage was not legal. She read the note and read it again. She didn't even know who had sent it because it had been placed on a table in her room. She worried about the content. Was it a joke? Did someone mean to frighten her? She knew there was bitter resentment against her. Just when she had decided it was an unpleasant joke, she received a second note. This time it was on her dressing table. The message was short, badly written, and poorly spelled. Did you take heed of my warning? She became very concerned and questioned her ladies about notes left around for her perusal. Each of them denied any knowledge. She wondered whether she should consult Edward but did nothing. At night she tossed in her bed, worried,

A third note appeared under her pillow. She shivered. She was scared; fear turned to anger. Whoever was sending these notes had access to her bedroom. This time the writer gave more information. King Edward was married secretly before he pretended to marry you. Your marriage is not legal. Your child will be a bastard!

Fear curled into a knot in the pit of her stomach. She had not even told Edward she was pregnant. What did the writer know? Was it true? Was Edward already married?

Elizabeth was determined to find out how the messages had found their way to her rooms. She interviewed each of her ladies individually. Not one of them admitted guilt. The ladies, too, were concerned. Someone was lying. Tension grew. There was one, however, who knew the truth. Lady Adelaide was the youngest. She had only served the queen for a short while. She had replaced her older sister Mary who had been dismissed by the queen because she had caught Edward's eye. Mary, disgraced, had been sent to a religious house. Mary was angry. The queen had been unfair. It was not her fault Edward was attracted to her. She had not encouraged him. Quite the reverse. She did all she could to keep out of his way. That had apparently amused him. He enjoyed a chase. It was unfortunate that Elizabeth had entered the room just as he had stolen a kiss. Elizabeth said nothing. She turned her back and waited for the embarrassed king to leave the room. Then she turned on Mary. Her words were as cold as ice. "You will prepare yourself to leave this evening."

Lady Mary had no idea what would happen to her. She felt it was so unfair. She had done nothing wrong. Elizabeth knew that it was probably true, but she arranged for the girl to be sent to a religious house out of the eye of Edward. Elizabeth invited Mary's younger sister Adelaide to take her place. That would placate their parents and relieve her conscience.

The Lady Mary was livid. She was determined to punish the queen, but she didn't know how. It was by chance that she had overheard one of the nun's speaking of Eleanor's plight. She had no idea who they were talking about, but she heard the words about Edward that rang bells in her ears. Edward had been involved in a secret marriage before Elizabeth Woodville had appeared on the scene. Was it true? She didn't know and didn't care. But if only she could whisper those words into Elizabeth's ear. How tormented she would be. How deliciously frightened.

It had taken months to persuade her sister to deliver the notes. She didn't tell her what was in them. What she didn't know, she couldn't tell. She simply begged her to help her revenge for the injustice done to her. The pain the queen had caused her.

Why shouldn't the queen suffer a little pain in retribution? Lady Mary would never know how much pain Queen Elizabeth would suffer. Nor would she ever understand the pain she had inflicted on so many others.

Lady Adelaide had carried out the errand magnificently. She selected each place with care, ensuring that no one observed her. It was a brilliant stroke of luck that she was able to place the last note under the queen's pillow. They had all left the rooms to go to dinner, but she had left a kerchief behind and hurried back to collect it. The queen's bedroom door was opened, and she observed the bed had been made. It took seconds to slip the note under a pillow. Elizabeth would not find it for hours; nevertheless, her heart had fluttered with excitement and fear. The queen was exceedingly angry and determined to find the culprit. The individual interview with each of her ladies was frightening. Lady Adelaide could feel her heart beating so hard she was surprised the queen could not hear it. When the queen asked her directly if she knew who had delivered the notes, she shook her head. "Do you know the content?" The question caught her by surprise. Adelaide was so pleased she could truthfully answer no. Elizabeth stared at her for what seemed like minutes. Then she dismissed her. She was convinced Adelaide was telling the truth.

Elizabeth sunk into a chair in despair. She had done all she could to solve the mystery. She wondered what would happen next. Clearly, this message was designed to topple her from the throne. She thought about her unborn child. She had told no one that a prince was on his way to the world. A male heir would surely stabilize her position. She had to know the truth. A smile spread over her face. Of course, there was one person she could trust to make sense of it all.

Chapter 4

In 1416 a baby girl, Jacquetta of Luxembourg, was born to Pierre de Luxembourg, Count of St. Pol, Conversano and Brienne, seigneur of Enghien and Vicomte of Lille. Her mother was Marguerite des Baux (or del Balzo in Italian). At the age of 17, she married the brother of Henry V, John Duke of Bedford. This beautiful, young bride was left a widow in September 1435, just two years after her marriage. Her husband had tried to leave her well-provided, but inheritance laws in England made it impossible. That is until King Henry VI allowed her the usual dower of one-third of Bedford's property. This agreement allowed her to return to England on the condition she obtain permission before remarrying. However, Jacquetta married Sir Richard Woodville without the king's permission. It was not acceptable for a woman of status to marry a man of little means. Jacquetta was forced to beg the king's pardon and pay a huge fine.

Jacquetta and her husband were chosen to escort King Henry VI's new bride Margaret of Anjou, from France to England for the wedding. Jacquettta became a high favourite of the new queen. The Woodville family were staunch supporters of the House of Lancaster in the War of the Roses, that is, until their daughter Elizabeth became Queen of England.

Queen Elizabeth was very close to her mother and often sought her advice. It was rumoured Jacquetta helped her daughter capture the king's heart. Now, she sat in a private room at the palace where Elizabeth had dropped the notes into her lap. If anyone could help her, it was her mother. Some claimed Jacquetta used magic to get what she wanted.

"Why didn't you show me these before?" Jacquetta spoke firmly to her daughter. Elizabeth shook her head.

"I thought it was some kind of joke, or maybe someone wanted to frighten me. But the third note," she shuddered, "the third note that is something else. Do you think it is true, mother? Would Edward have deceived me?"

Jacquetta rolled her eyes. "If it suited him, he would. Have you asked him?"

"Heavens no." Elizabeth was quick to reply. "I was too frightened to. Supposing he said yes."

Jacquetta laughed. "Well, you have learned something. Even if he was in a contract before he married you, what would he achieve by admitting it?"

Elizabeth's eyes opened wide. "Do you think he was?" The coil of fear tightened in her stomach.

Jacquetta shrugged her shoulders. "Anything is possible. It is a blessing you are with child." Elizabeth put her hand to her stomach. Of course, her mother would know. She smiled. "A son for Edward." Jacquetta shook her head, "Not this time, dear, a daughter first." Elizabeth was disappointed for a moment, but a daughter, that would be a new experience. She already had two sons. A daughter would be delightful. Perhaps a son would follow. Her thoughts flew back to her problem. She sighed.

"We need to discover who this supposed woman is."

Jacquetta frowned. "That shouldn't be difficult. Edward is easily tempted by a pretty face. You know he bedded a young woman just before he met you. A pretty young woman, I am told, but of course, she didn't last. The silly girl was too keen to get into his bed. She did get a daughter out of him, so I am informed." Elizabeth pouted. She didn't want to hear this. Jacquetta gave her wrist a playful slap.

"Don't be silly. She is the past. You are the present and future. I've told you, Elizabeth, you have power. You cannot afford the luxury of jealousy. Use your power to keep him *bewitched.*" The emphasis on the word bewitched made them both laugh. Already rumours had circulated that Elizabeth, with the help of her mother, had bewitched Edward into secretly marrying her.

"But what should I do, mother? It frightens me to death. If there is any truth in it, and this person speaks out, I could lose Edward, and my children would be... bastards."

Jacquetta patted her daughter's hand. "You have done what you should. You have told me. I will find out the truth and deal with it. You are not to be involved. Leave these notes with me. It shouldn't be difficult to solve this little problem." Elizabeth felt a sense of relief. Her mother was not worried and was convinced she could eradicate the problem. Suddenly, she felt the flutter of a butterfly in her lower abdomen – "the quickening," she whispered. My baby has quickened.

Jacquetta had not told her daughter that, indeed, she had heard rumours that there was an alleged marriage between Edward and another woman before he married Elizabeth. In fact, she had several contacts prepared to name the woman. She had learned that the lady concerned was not a commoner but, in fact, a daughter of an earl. As such, she could have the resources to challenge Edward's marriage to Elizabeth. The question was why she had not.

Jacquetta had thought that perhaps Warwick had spread the rumour for spite. He had worked hard to arrange an alliance with the French. Just when he thought he had succeeded and found a suitable bride, Edward told him he was already married. The French would never forgive the insult. Warwick was furious. It wouldn't surprise her if he sought to destroy the marriage as revenge. But her intuition told her it wasn't Warwick.

Jacquetta was an intelligent woman. She understood victory is won by the element of surprise. She would confront Edward, catch him off guard. He would no doubt reveal the truth.

Edward watched Jacquetta approach him. Although she had birthed many children, she had not aged. She was still a very beautiful woman, well-educated and powerful but mysterious. He was never quite at ease with her. He was aware that she had once been sister-in-law to King Henry V, but the Duke of Bedford had died within a couple of years of their marriage. She was a favourite of Queen Margaret of Anjou, his enemy. She was a very determined woman who defied King Henry and married beneath her without the permission of the crown. However, she had sought and been given a pardon. There were rumours she used magic, but Edward preferred not to believe it.

"Your majesty," Jacquetta gave a deep curtsey. Her throaty voice, with just a slight European accent, fascinated him. He acknowledged her and invited her to sit with him. He didn't need to be told she would prefer those close to him to be gone; he dismissed them. Her smile thanked him. There was no need for words. But her words, when they were spoken, stunned him.

"I understand you have deceived us all. You were already married to a noble lady when you supposedly married my daughter." As much as he tried to keep calm, the blood drained from his face. Jacquetta smiled inwardly. Yes, she had caught him off guard. She leaned back in her chair, watching his face work, searching for words. Finally, the words came with an effort of haughtiness. "My Lady, watch what you say. You speak treason?"

Jacquetta didn't raise a hair; she simply smiled. "Edward, I am on your side. You are married to my daughter, the queen. I want it to remain that way." Edward had faced fierce opponents on the battlefield, but he had never felt as scared as he did just then. Jacquetta stared into his eyes as if searching his soul. Thoughts of powers she might have raced through his head. What should he do? What could he do? Should he call his guards? She would think him weak and laugh. Elizabeth would never forgive him. As if she had read his mind, she softened her voice. 'You do know Elizabeth is with child?"

His expression revealed he didn't know. Joy was immediately replaced by fear. Was his son to be a bastard?

Jacquetta simply put a finger to her lips. "Who is she?" She looked straight into his frightened eyes. "Why didn't she challenge your marriage to Elizabeth?"

A vision of Eleanor appeared before him. He saw her dear face, tears wetting her cheeks as she spoke the words, *"Isn't it enough my husband died fighting a war for the throne of England? You leave me homeless, your majesty."* He had promised so much and delivered so little. Sorrow, guilt, and pity filled his heart.

"She will never do anything to hurt me,' his voice was just a whisper, but such tenderness surprised Jacquetta. She had her answer. The rumour was true. Her daughter's marriage was in jeopardy. She must act.

She didn't ask Edward any more about the woman. She had her sources to find out who she was.

Edward spoke. "Does Elizabeth know? I don't want Elizabeth to hear anything."

Jacquetta stood ready to leave. "She has heard rumours but thinks someone is trying to frighten her. I am not sure you will be able to keep it from her or if that would be the best option. If she knows, she will be in a better position to defend you. She is a strong woman and willing to fight those who cross her."

Edward wondered if her words were a warning or meant to comfort. Jacquetta leaned forward and whispered, "You are not a weak man Edward. You will know what to do. Forewarned is acknowledged her and invited her to sit with him. He didn't need to be told she would prefer those close to him to be gone; he dismissed them. Her smile thanked him. There was no need for words. But her words, when they were spoken, stunned him.

"I understand you have deceived us all. You were already married to a noble lady when you supposedly married my daughter." As much as he tried to keep calm, the blood drained from his face. Jacquetta smiled inwardly. Yes, she had caught him off guard. She leaned back in her chair, watching his face work, searching for words. Finally, the words came with an effort of haughtiness. "My Lady, watch what you say. You speak treason?"

Jacquetta didn't raise a hair; she simply smiled. "Edward, I am on your side. You are married to my daughter, the queen. I want it to remain that way." Edward had faced fierce opponents on the battlefield, but he had never felt as scared as he did just then. Jacquetta stared into his eyes as if searching his soul. Thoughts of powers she might have raced through his head. What should he do? What could he do? Should he call his guards? She would think him weak and laugh. Elizabeth would never forgive him. As if she had read his mind, she softened her voice. 'You do know Elizabeth is with child?"

His expression revealed he didn't know. Joy was immediately replaced by fear. Was his son to be a bastard?

Jacquetta simply put a finger to her lips. "Who is she?" She looked straight into his frightened eyes. "Why didn't she challenge your marriage to Elizabeth?"

A vision of Eleanor appeared before him. He saw her dear face, tears wetting her cheeks as she spoke the words, *"Isn't it enough my husband died fighting a war for the throne of England? You leave me homeless, your majesty."* He had promised so much and delivered so little. Sorrow, guilt, and pity filled his heart.

"She will never do anything to hurt me,' his voice was just a whisper, but such tenderness surprised Jacquetta. She had her answer. The rumour was true. Her daughter's marriage was in jeopardy. She must act.

She didn't ask Edward any more about the woman. She had her sources to find out who she was.

Edward spoke. "Does Elizabeth know? I don't want Elizabeth to hear anything."

Jacquetta stood ready to leave. "She has heard rumours but thinks someone is trying to frighten her. I am not sure you will be able to keep it from her or if that would be the best option. If she knows, she will be in a better position to defend you. She is a strong woman and willing to fight those who cross her."

Edward wondered if her words were a warning or meant to comfort. Jacquetta leaned forward and whispered, "You are not a weak man Edward. You will know what to do. Forewarned is forearmed." She curtsied and left.

Edward watched her go. He dwelt on the words she had spoken. "Not a weak man…know what to do…forewarned is forearmed. " Was she expecting him to get rid of Eleanor? That was not his intention.

He wondered why Elizabeth had not spoken to him about the matter herself. Why had she talked to her mother first? It was not like her. She had demonstrated her fiery nature many times if he dared glance at another woman. Look what happened when she, unfortunately, witnessed him having a little fun with one of the ladies, just a little kiss.

Chapter 5

Edward was surprised to hear that Eleanor no longer lived at Fenny Compton. Nor was she staying with her sister at Framlington Castle. Finally, he discovered she was living at East Hall, Kenninghall, Norfolk. He decided to journey there alone. This was to be a private meeting. He was not quite sure what he was going to do. The bell made a resounding chime that echoed throughout the building. He waited impatiently and was about to ring the bell again when he heard footsteps. Slowly the heavy door began to open, and to his surprise, standing before him was a nun. She stared, then her mouth dropped in recognition, and she quickly dropped into a low curtsey. Edward stepped forward, querulously gesturing her to rise. He brushed past her. Where is the Lady

Eleanor? Eleanor was in a room close by and recognised the king's voice. Could it be Edward calling on her after all this time? A multitude of emotions overwhelmed her. She stood up and sat again. The nun raced ahead of the king to warn Eleanor of his arrival. Eleanor watched as he stepped hesitantly into the room. She nodded to the nun, assuring her that all was right, slowly stood and made a deep curtsey.

Edward watched the nun as she left the room, then, moving forward, quickly clasped Eleanor's hands. They felt cold to him, but his heart stirred as his eyes met hers. He still felt the passion, and he was sure she did too. She withdrew her hands and looked at him coldly. Uncertain what to say in her confusion she just stood staring, hardly believing he was there. How many times had she longed for this moment, but not now! Oh no, not now! He had taken another wife without even talking to her about it. What could he possibly want? There was nothing left for them.

She recalled the disbelief and joy she had felt when she realised she was pregnant and how it soon changed to anger and fear when she discovered that Edward had betrayed her. How fervently she had prayed for guidance. Should she tell Edward that she was carrying his child, a son? How would he react? Would he return to her and tell the world she was his wife? Their child would be his legitimate heir. Then she remembered the whispers regarding his intimate relationship with his cousin Henry Beaufort,

Duke of Somerset. His denial - it was not serious - just politics. How angry she had become. He considered that a reasonable and acceptable excuse. She had tried to ignore the talk of a new romance that followed Somerset's betrayal. A romance that was rumoured involved a daughter. Her prayers became angry, and God understood. She would not challenge his illegal marriage. He would never have the joy of his son. She could not live with a man who was so morally deficient.

She had thought she hated him, but seeing him in front of her, she knew that hate was out of the question despite his infidelity. She wanted to tell him about the child she had born. His child - a son. The wonderful gift of an heir, an heir she had not been able to give Thomas and Lord Sudeley. Oh! How bitterly she had regretted she had not had a son for Thomas. She had suspected she was with child when the Duke of Norfolk announced at the dinner table Edward was married to Elizabeth Woodville. Eleanor was devastated. She told no one, not even her sister, but had returned to Fenny Compton until she was sure.

"I don't know what to say to you, Eleanor." She started. His voice came from afar. She realised he was speaking to her.

"There is nothing you can say, Edward. Your actions have said it all. What did you expect me to do? Run to Warwick screaming, 'You were mine?' Cry out to the Archbishop, 'He married me first?' You didn't even have the courtesy to tell me yourself."

Edward began to fumble. He sat in a nearby chair. This was not what he expected.

"Why this visit?" Eleanor spoke bitterly. "Are you going to confiscate the property you gave me - to give it to your make-believe wife?" Edward winced. The comment stung. He hung his head and spoke in a raspy voice.

"Eleanor, forgive me. I have behaved badly" Eleanor raised her eyebrows. "Behaved badly! Badly is too kind." She spat the words. She felt a lump in her throat and fought back her tears.

Edward looked up sharply. "Be careful, Eleanor. You are speaking to your king. Even as the words tumbled from his lips, he realised how foolish he sounded

Eleanor lowered her voice and spoke very slowly, looking into his eyes defiantly. "Edward, there is nothing you could do that will hurt me more than you have already." Edward coughed. His chest tightened. He felt a tearing pain, a stabbing.

"Someone has been sending notes to my …to the Queen, warning her that her marriage isn't legal, her children will be bastards."

Eleanor smiled. "Well, that is a truth. Perhaps she should be warned."

"I warn you, Eleanor, if it is you! God knows! I'll put an end to it."

Eleanor shook her head in disbelief. "You, my husband, why you don't know me at all, do you? I would not stoop so low. Is it not obvious? I do not intend to challenge your invalid marriage. If I had, I might have told you about the birth of our son." She bit her lip. The words had slipped out."

He gripped the side of the chair. "What did you say? We have a son?" He threw himself back in the chair and gave a strained laugh. "You are lying!" His words angered Eleanor. She wanted to hurt him. She wanted him to feel some of the pain she had. Her words were cold. "Yes, Edward, we had a son. I didn't get a chance to tell you I was with child before I heard of your marriage. Then it was too late. You will never have a son on the throne, Edward. You will never meet my son." She put a hand to her face; her cheeks were burning.

Edward stood. He towered over her. She didn't flinch.

"Is my son alive?" His words were surprisingly gentle. She looked at him, wondering what she should say. Had she put her son in danger?

Edward saw her hesitate. She had never lied to him. He knew she would not answer. He had come to silence her about their marriage; now it was crucial that the queen, his wife, did not find out he had a son who was legally his heir. He felt a sense of panic as a thought flashed through his mind. Would Elizabeth be capable of giving him a son? He put his hands to his face. What a mess!

Eleanor felt his despair. She should be delighted. Countless tears spent because of him, yet she felt such empathy for this man, her husband, and realised she still loved him so dearly. She stretched out a hand. "I will never challenge your marriage, Edward. You need have no fear for the queen and your future children. The secret will go to my grave with me."

Edward took a deep breath. He fought the prick in his eyes. Men don't cry. Shame, sorrow, and unhappiness filled his being. How could he have treated her so? He reached out and took her in his arms. She stiffened for a moment. His eyes met hers, and she saw his love. He bent forward and gently kissed her, long and tenderly. They both knew it was the last time their lips would meet.

The birth of Edward Plantagenet de Wigmore was a closely guarded secret. Eleanor wanted him to have a normal life, at least until he came of age, and to have an excellent education. She was not interested in him becoming king, his birthright. If he ever discovered his true identity, it would be his choice whether he pursued it. In the meantime, to protect his safety, Eleanor called him Giles Plantagenet.

Eleanor had provided for her son's keep and education through her very generous donations to the religious house Corpus Christi College. Dr. John Botwright, the master of Corpus Christi College, with whom she negotiated her endowment, had been very kind. When Giles was born, Dr. Botwright made arrangements to assist

Eleanor with her wishes for him to be cared for by the religious house. Her sister was his godmother, and Eleanor had trusted Elizabeth to secretly care for her son if anything should happen to her. Eleanor regretted even mentioning him to Edward and prayed for his safety. His life was in the hands of God, and circumstances suggest that for a while at least, young Giles was in no danger.

Jacquetta had her spies. She had discovered the secret queen was Lady Eleanor Boetler. She knew the king had been to see Eleanor, but he hadn't spoken of it since his return. She had made one or two attempts to get him to talk, but he brushed her questions aside. Finally, he said testily, "You have no need to be concerned about her; she has vowed to remain silent."

Elizabeth found her husband had recently become increasingly moody. She had thought that once she had told him of their coming child, he would be overjoyed, but he had hardly acknowledged it. Elizabeth was still angry about the news her mother had told her. Edward had given his mistress a daughter. Her mother had become impatient with her. "It was before your time. Do not dwell on it." Elizabeth couldn't help herself. She spoke of it one evening when she and Edward were alone. He had glowered at her and remarked she just needed to get on with giving him a son. It fuelled her anger. Not only was he unashamed of his licentious behaviour, but he didn't even try to hide it.

A few months later, Elizabeth gave birth to a daughter. Edward was not surprised. Jacquetta told him there was plenty of time for a son, it would happen, but Edward remembered Eleanor's words. No son of his would gain the throne. He tried to convince himself that she had spoken in anger, but it did not prevent him from worrying. He had thought about the son she had mentioned. Their son. He wanted to know more, but what good would it do? He did not need to acknowledge he was his son, just ensure he had a title and wealth as such a son of his deserved. He was, after all, his legitimate heir. Eleanor had not confirmed he lived, but why would she protect him if he were dead? He wondered if her sister, Elizabeth knew of his existence. They were very close.

He also thought about the letters sent to his queen. Eleanor had not actually said she did not have anything to do with them, but then why would she? If she wanted the secret known, she could simply challenge the marriage. It had to be someone else who sent the letters.

Jacquetta realised Edward was not going to enlighten them about what happened when he visited Eleanor. She had thought that he would organise something to get rid of her. Perhaps he might yet, but he had apparently loved Elainor once, and it wasn't a good idea to fan that love again. No, she would need to deal with her. She tossed ideas around in her head about how she could become acquainted with Eleanor without suspicion. She put her spies at work. Finally, they reported some interesting news.

Eleanor was an active patroness of Corpus Christs College, Cambridge. She also had, until recently, lived in a religious house in Norwich – namely, the Carmelite Friars. Eleanor was a very generous, religious lady. Jacquetta had no doubt that the nuns would be very protective of their lady. They might also know her secrets. They could easily believe that exposing the king could be to Eleanor's advantage and encourage her to speak up. That would not do. She would need to ensure that would not happen. Jacquetta gave a satisfied smile. Intuitively, she knew she was on to something.

Chapter 6

Eleanor listened to her sister Elizabeth talk about the grand preparations for Princess Margaret's wedding to the Duke of Burgundy. It was a warm, sunny day in May. Elizabeth had found some time to visit Eleanor but warned her that she was so engaged it would probably be July before she saw her sister again.

"I suppose it is hardly surprising that you are the only one in the family who has not been commanded to assume an honorary role in connection with the marriage of Princess Margaret, but I wish you had been included." Eleanor was very pleased to remain invisible. She wondered who had made the decision to deny her the honour; was it Edward or even Elizabeth, his queen?

Elizabeth, Duchess of Norfolk, was honoured she was chosen

to escort Princess Margaret on her wedding journey. She was to head the princess's suit of attendants together with a large train of her own. It was all very exciting; she would witness the exchange of promises and the formal marriage ceremony. She sometimes felt dizzy with the huge responsibility. It took every moment of her waking day. She sighed, "You have no idea how demanding it is to organise my own wardrobe." Eleanor smiled. "I am sure you have plenty of advisors."

It was a relief when Elizabeth had left. Eleanor had urgent business she needed to attend. She had written to William Catesby, a relative by marriage to her father's niece. The family often approached him for legal advice. She had indicated that the business was a matter of urgency. He had promised to attend to her within two to three weeks. She expected him any day, and it was a relief her sister had returned to her busy life. She did not want to involve her.

Two days later, on 15th May, Catesby arrived. There began the usual chatter of family and the pending marriage of Princess Margaret. In the late afternoon, they sat in the library, a smaller room than others and furnished with a huge desk and several comfortable chairs,

"I hardly know where to begin, William." Eleanor, usually so calm, looked agitated. Catesby simply smiled reassuringly. "The truth is, I fear for my life." The words exploded into the room.

Catesby looked across at Eleanor, hardly believing what he had just heard. "Are you sure I am the person you need to speak to?" he asked gently. He rubbed his chin, looking at her intently. Lady Eleanor was not the kind of person to be dramatic. He had known her for some years, and she was always in control of her emotions.

"No. You are the person I need. I can trust you. I want you to prepare a deed of gift of Fenny Compton to my sister Elizabeth, effective immediately." Catesby waited.

'Yes, immediately," Eleanor repeated as if confirming the idea to herself. "The matter is urgent."

Catesby listened but made no comment. He was sure there was more to come. Eleanor sat quietly, watching him, waiting for him to speak. She began tapping her fingers on the arm of the chair.

Finally, he spoke. "Are you requiring a will?" he asked. She hesitated. "No, yes, I don't know. I must get my affairs in order, William. I do not know how long I have left, but they won't let me live. Not now she knows." She put her hands to her face; he could hear soft sobs."

"Eleanor, who won't let you live? Who is she?" He stood from his chair and knelt beside her. "This sounds serious, but you need to be more explicit."

She removed her hands from her face. It was damp where she had brushed away her tears. What did it matter now if she told

Catesby? She had believed she was safe, provided she did not challenge the king's new marriage. However, someone had sent letters to the queen claiming Edward already had a queen. This new marriage was illegal. Any children would be bastards.

Edward's surprise visit after all these years made her nervous. He came to threaten her but realised she had no knowledge of the letters. Who, then, was the culprit? She knew Edward was scared. A scared man was capable of anything.

Eleanor moved forward on her chair, looked quickly over her shoulder, then, satisfied, whispered into Catesby's ear. 'William, what I am about to tell you is so confidential it would risk your life if you ever spoke of it to anyone." He looked startled. "Surely it cannot be that bad?" he replied with a strangled laugh.

She told him of her marriage just after Edward became king. They exchanged vows in front of a priest, but Edward wanted it to be a secret until he had told Warwick.

Catesby gaped. Eleanor was telling him she was the true Queen of England. Was it some kind of joke?

"You were married to King Edward by a priest?" Eleanor heard the disbelief in his voice. She stared at him defiantly, "Yes, it is true." Catesby stood up.

"My God, Eleanor. You can't speak of such a thing. Does anyone else know?" she watched beads of perspiration break out on his forehead. Perhaps she had been wrong to tell him.

"My sister, the Duchess of Norfolk, celebrated the wedding feast with us." He looked at her blankly.

"Elizabeth knows. What about your mother? I realise she has passed, but why didn't your family do something to support you? My God, you are the daughter of an Earl. You have an influential family. Why did none of them give you support? It is beyond belief!"

After a moment's thought, his face lit up. "Warwick, your uncle. Why didn't he step in? He would have preferred you rather than a Woodville queen. "Eleanor shook her head. She had often wondered what Warwick would have done if he was told. It infuriated him that Edward had ruined the chance of an alliance with France. She looked at Catesby, his face red with frustration, pleased she had not told him about their child. But she did speak of Edward's visit. She mentioned that he had told her every day was a nightmare since the queen had received the letters. She was like a dog with a bone. She would not rest until she had found out the truth and who had sent the letters. Edward had even warned her life would be in jeopardy if she dared to challenge him.

Eleanor spoke with frustration." Don't you see? I had no option. I could not challenge the marriage. Edward is very powerful. How would it be if I failed? What would my prospects be? Besides, why would I want to remain married to a man who had betrayed me? I had heard of his dalliance with Somerset. I loved him, and trusted him, but his behaviour disgusted me. Elizabeth Woodville might be prepared to look the other way, but that was not the life for me."

Catesby did not reply. Once, he would have argued she should have fought for her rights. She was the Queen of England. He was convinced he could have argued her case if told about it at the time. But perhaps she was right. What kind of life would it have been for her? Edward could not be trusted. He had failed her. The king had spoken of a threat to her life.

Catesby let out a long sigh. "You did the right thing, Eleanor. You would have no hope in challenging the king now unless you could get the priest to speak up as a witness. You can be sure the priest is rewarded well to keep silent. Your reputation would be in ruin. Yes, you were sensible not to challenge." He moved to the table; a thought struck him. He asked if there had been any attempt on her life. She answered she was sure someone was trying to poison her. She had noticed there were one or two new faces in the household staff. When she questioned her ladies, they said they were replacements for staff who had moved on. They had believed she knew about it. Then her health had suddenly deteriorated. She had fits of vomiting and diarrhea followed by an excruciating muscle cramp. She suspected poisoning. Eleanor shrugged her shoulders. Perhaps she was becoming neurotic, but since mentioning her fears to her lady and only eating when others ate the same, symptoms stopped. She gave a little laugh. "But they will get me; I am sure about that."

Catesby sat at the table. "Come, we will do as you wish and get your affairs in order."

"Edward gave me a property in Wiltshire. The manor of Oare-under-Savernake. Can I give that to Elizabeth?"

"My. My." Catesby looked quite cheerful. "That will be interesting. How will the king explain that? He laughed. "I will look at the deed and see what I can do."

Catesby was true to his word. He drew up the deed of gift in favour of Elizabeth, Duchess of Norfolk. Catesby advised Eleanor to sign it as 'lately wife of Thomas Boetler Knight, now deceased. Fenny Compton conveyed to Elizabeth absolutely with immediate effect. It was signed 4th June 1468. Elizabeth was also granted the reversion of all her Wiltshire property.

Eleanor breathed a sigh of relief. Catesby had witnessed all her papers, and everything was in order in the event of her death.

Eleanor slept more peacefully at night than she had for months.

While Elizabeth was enjoying her time with the new Duchess of Burgundy, her sister waited for death. She no longer vomited or had cramps. She made sure only her most faithful lady prepared her food.

Eleanor awoke suddenly on the night of 30th June. A beautiful apparition was present. Was it an angel? She stared in disbelief at the image standing in the light of the moon. A white gown in what looked like the finest silk made a slight rustle as the angel moved toward the bed. Golden hair touched Eleanor's face as the angel bent as if to give a gentle kiss. An unusual but exquisite aroma filled the air. Too late, Eleanor realised who she was. She tried to sit up, but a hand firmly pushed her back at the same time, covering her face with a soft muslin cloth. The pungent fragrance had an immediate effect. There was no struggle, no pain, Eleanor quickly slipped into unconsciousness, and within minutes she drew her last breath.

The angel smiled. There would be no evidence, no blame, and no more threat.

King Edward was not surprised to hear of Lady Eleanor's death. He had been expecting it. No blame could be put on him. He was very angry. She posed no threat. He was sure of that. Didn't the fools realise her murder did not solve the problem, only posed more. His marriage to Elizabeth was still illegal, and Sweet Jesus, he was not about to admit it was true. Stillington had been rewarded enough for his part. His lips were sealed. He frowned. There would be a need for chancery to determine what property Eleanor held on the day of her death. In frustration, he tapped his fingers on the arm of his chair. God's oath that was a problem in itself. What did she do about her property in Wiltshire? That could cause tongues to wag.

William Catesby stared at the parchment with King Edward's seal firmly attached. It was a summons to court. He felt a flutter of nerves. What did the king want from him? He had only recently heard the news of Lady Eleanor's death. It was said she died peacefully in her sleep. He swallowed. An inner knowing whispered Edward is aware you know his secret. But no. He had taken great care with the wording on the legal documents he had created at her instructions. Nothing could suggest that he knew anything about her relationship with the king. In fact, he had insisted that she sign her name as 'lately wife of Thomas Boetler Knight, now deceased.' There could be no suggestion that she was the wife of King Edward. He paced the room. A knot of fear formed in his stomach. It was crucial Edward remained oblivious to his knowledge of their marriage. How glad he was that he had told no one about the enormous secret. He recalled Lady Eleanor's words. "William, I am about to tell you something that would risk your life if you ever told anyone." He stopped pacing - a thought struck him. Did it cost her life? He began pacing backward and forward again, this time more urgently. It was imperative he push such thought from his mind. It wouldn't do! It wouldn't do at all. His eye caught the summons he had cast aside. One did not ignore a summons from the king. He must make haste. He knew the king was at Windsor. He could be there by tomorrow.

Edward was not quite sure what he wanted from Catesby. He had been told that the man had completed her legal papers. Would she have broken their secret? He narrowed his eyes, but he remembered the honesty on her face when she vowed she would not challenge the marriage. He had nothing to fear. He trusted her. Perhaps it was more than he deserved. A flash of anger made him clench his fist. He didn't believe Eleanor had died naturally in her sleep. She had been murdered, and he had a good idea who was responsible. Elizabeth, his wife, or her mother, Jacquetta, probably both. How did they achieve it? Magic? Sorcery? Perhaps it was better not to know. God forbid they ever got knowledge of his son. The thought of his son caused a smile to cross his face. How he wished Eleanor had told him more. One day he would find him. He was determined to make him a baron and give him the wealth a son of his deserved. For now, he would keep quiet about him. Elizabeth would not rest until she was rid of him. Perhaps it would be different when she had produced a son. His thoughts were interrupted. William Catesby had arrived.

King Edward had decided to talk to Catesby without a witness. It was safer that way. He watched him closely as he bowed before him. Catesby accepted the seat and waited for the king to speak. Edward considered him for a while. The man appeared perfectly at ease. But why shouldn't he if he knew nothing?

"I trust you had a good journey." He eyed Catesby steadily. Catesby nodded, "I did thank you, your majesty." His response was short. The king did not summons him to ask about his journey. His strategy was to say as little as possible. Less can be construed with silence. Too many involved themselves in nervous chatter that only got them into trouble. Edward coughed. He shifted his feet, then spoke. "We were very sad to hear of our subject, Lady Eleanor's recent death. So unexpected." Catesby agreed. "Indeed, your majesty. She was so young."

"And you, Catesby, I understand you were her legal advisor."

"That is true, your majesty. I have advised her and other members of her family for a number of years." Catesby wondered where the king's conversation was heading.

"Yes. Yes." The king stood, and Catesby immediately followed suit. "We understand you were with her quite recently when she wished to gift Fenny Compton manor to her sister. Immediately I believe?"

"That is correct, your majesty. It was early June when she made the request." The king bit his lip, his eyes not leaving Catesby's.

"Did you not think that was quite strange? Why would she wish to give the Duchess of Norfolk her property?

"It is perfectly natural for a widowed woman with no children to wish to have her affairs in order…" Edward interrupted. "But, 'absolutely with immediate effect'. Didn't that strike you as strange?" Catesby stiffened. "It is not my business to question my client. Lady Eleanor was of sound mind. I believed she was capable of making her own decision." Edward noted Catesby's defensive tone. He tried another tactic.

"Do you think she believed she was dying?" Catesby was shocked by the question. His stomach churned. Edward responded immediately. "My dear man, how thoughtless of me. You have journeyed far." He turned and shouted for his man to bring refreshments.

Catesby waited for the king to seat himself again, then gladly accepted the offered chair.

"And did you?" The king began again. For a brief moment, Catesby was confused. "Did you think Lady Eleanor thought she was dying?" The question was important. Edward wanted an answer. Catesby was well aware it was a pointed question. Edward was really asking if Eleanor thought her life was in danger. If he answered in the affirmative, it would suggest that she had talked to him and maybe told him she was frightened for her life. That would lead to the obvious question, why? He had to make sure that line of thinking was avoided. It was a cat-and-mouse game. He took a gamble.

"I did ask her that very question. She laughed and said the

question was absurd. She was very well, and it was not my business why she had decided to make it a gift to her sister. I felt quite chastised, I can tell you." The king's man entered with refreshments. Catesby watched as a board was quickly set up, and various kinds of small pies, cold meats, sauces, and fruit were piled in the dishes. His stomach rumbled again.

Edward laughed and reached for a chunk of delicious-smelling white bread to dip in the sauce. The aroma from the jug of ale made Catsby realise that, yes, his churning stomach was telling him he hadn't eaten, and he was gasping for a swig of that ale.

Edward was satisfied that Eleanor had not broken his trust. At least Catesby didn't appear to believe she was frightened for her life. He, on the other hand, thought differently. He wondered what had happened to make her act the way she did. What had those women in his life done to make her realise her life was in danger?

However, it was clear he needed to have a word in a few people's ears before the result of the inquisition post-mortem to determine what properties she had held. He was well aware Eleanor had not received a royal licence to transfer Fenny Compton to her sister, but he would ignore that for the time being. It was something he would hold over Elizabeth, Duchess of Norfolk, to keep her silenced. However, Lord Sudeley would pay. He no longer had to consider Eleanor's father-in-law; now, she was dead. He was a traitor, a faithful Lancastrian. He would pay and pay dearly.

Chapter 7

Elizabeth, Duchess of Norfolk, arrived home to the news that her sister had died. She felt suddenly cold. Her sister was well when she had left her, to die suddenly, with no explanation raised questions. How convenient it should happen when her friends and family were out of the country, engaged in Princess Margaret's wedding. Was it a deliberate act that Eleanor had not been included in the wedding plans?

Elizabeth fondly remembered her last visit to Eleanor at Kenninghall. It pleased her that Eleanor desired to live there, a manor not far from where she lived herself. She was well aware of her sister's devotion to the Carmelite lay oblates; she had been a patroness for years, but she had been surprised Eleanor had spoken, just a few weeks earlier of her wish to be buried in the choir of the Carmelite Priory church in Norwich. Eleanor had been quietly persistent that Elizabeth take note of how she should go about the arrangements. Elizabeth recalled her words, spoken quite urgently, "Speak to Father McMannus. He will arrange it. Promise me you will do that." Elizabeth had felt Eleanor's eyes searching her soul for assurance.

She leaned forward and took her sister's hand. "Eleanor, what ails you? You are well?"

Eleanor twisted her lip, "Yes, I am well, but life is so unpredictable." She had withdrawn her hand, brightened her tone, and asked about the gowns Elizabeth had decided to wear at the royal wedding. It made sense now. Eleanor feared for her life.

Elizabeth followed the coffin as it passed beneath the beautiful archway of the great west doorway. She alone accompanied it. She knew Eleanor would have wanted it that way, particularly as their mother had recently died. She felt a sudden bitterness toward Edward as she watched the coffin journey toward her resting place. Her sister was still so young. Intuitively, she knew Edward was to blame. He may not have committed the actual deed, but he was responsible for the outcome. She tightened her lips, imagining how relieved the king and queen would be, knowing that Eleanor would never be able to challenge their marriage, believing they were safe. She wondered what part they had played in Eleanor's death.

Her mind drifted to walking with Warwick at the wedding of Princess Margaret. She heard the contempt in his voice when he spoke of King Edward.

"My oath! He is an ungrateful worm. He wouldn't be on the throne if I hadn't paved the way for him! Curses on him!" Warwick gave a grunt and spat on the ground. Then he grunted again before he spoke. "He did all he could to prevent my daughter Isabel from marrying his brother George. His voice rose a decimal. "Can you imagine such ingratitude? You would have thought that was the least he could do." Warwick gave an ugly laugh. "But we were too smart for him. They married in Calais. I wonder when he will hear that news."

Elizabeth shook her head. "You took a great risk, my Lord. I heard you got your revenge." Warwick smirked, then gave her a sly look.

"He has no idea how much he will regret turning his back on me. His loyalty is now to the Woodvilles. Lancastrians, the lot of them. Can't be trusted, couldn't be loyal to their own – switched sides when they thought they could thrust their snouts into the trough. Richard Woodville, the father of the whore, is his favourite. Forgotten what he owes me. All I've done for him. You know he's made him an Earl! Warwick screwed up his face and spat on the ground again. "He'll regret it. Just wait and see. He has a big surprise coming his way. That'll wipe the smug smile off his face."

Remembering Warwick's words gave Elizabeth a delightful sense of satisfaction that Edward was to suffer. She felt certain her sister was murdered. She found it difficult to resist the temptation to voice her suspicions in the hearing of Warwick and even the Duke of Clarence but realised it was foolish to even think her thoughts, let alone verbalise them. Nevertheless, anger and a sense of injustice that her sister had been so badly treated caused her to be heedless in their company.

There was one matter that Elizabeth had never shown imprudence. That related to her nephew Giles. She had made a solemn promise to Eleanor that she would never disclose to anyone the truth about the beautiful son Eleanor had given birth not long after she had learned of Edward's invalid marriage to Elizabeth Woodville. The baby was premature, but he was strong despite the belief he would not last the night. Elizabeth had found a wet nurse. Amazingly, the woman who had nearly died with shame, who berated herself for giving birth to a child out of wedlock, a child who died within hours, was the same woman who unknowingly saved the life of a tiny prince. The wet nurse, who provided the life-saving sustenance, never knew that the babe who suckled from her breasts was the son of the King of England.

The birth of Edward Plantagenet de Wigmore was a closely guarded secret. Eleanor was aware that if it became known he was the king's legitimate son, his life could be in danger. She wanted him to have a normal life, at least until he came of age, and to have an excellent education. She was not interested in him becoming king, his birthright. It should be his choice. To protect his identity, Eleanor called him Giles Plantagenet.

A few months after the funeral, William Catesby called on Elizabeth, Duchess of Norfolk, at Framlington Castle. She was sitting by the window in one of several large wooden chairs with cushions made from heavy tapestries and silk. Catesby noted her pale face and black smudges under her eyes. She beckoned him to a vacant chair opposite her. He sat and offered condolences for the death of her sister Lady Eleanor. She nodded and thanked him. It was difficult to keep her dignity; the pain was still raw.

"Your sister gifted you Fenny Compton absolutely with immediate effect 4th June last." He saw her look of surprise. He leaned toward, almost whispering. "Eleanor told me you knew about her relationship with King Edward. Elizabeth eyed him steadily. She was reluctant to say anything. Then intrigued asked. "Why would Eleanor gift me, Fenny Compton, with immediate effect? Catesby saw she was confused. He leaned forward again. "I believe she was fearful for her life. She wanted to ensure you received the manor and the property in Wiltshire." He tightened his lips. "I shouldn't, but I can tell you that someone of power has a hidden agenda." Elizabeth raised her eyebrows. "I have read the report of the Inquisition post-mortem. Griff and Burton Dassett have reverted to Lord Sudeley, but the king has confiscated them. The interesting thing is there is no mention of Fenny Compton or of the grant of reversion of the Wiltshire properties. It seems his majesty desires that you keep them." His tone changed. "Be wary, Elizabeth. The king is clearly aware you know too much. He may be wondering if Eleanor spoke to you of her fears."

A tear had travelled over Elizabeth's cheek. "I am sure she was murdered." Her voice was harsh. "She didn't tell me she feared her life, and perhaps that is because it all happened when I was at the royal wedding. It was very convenient that all her family was out of the way." Catesby looked up sharply. "Take care what you say, Elizabeth. There are those who will be watching you very carefully. Don't give them the opportunity to harm you." Catesby wished he could protect her. He had been her father's legal advisor for years. But there was only so much he could do, and he was certain the king, and probably the queen, would prefer she was not around.

Catesby refused the invitation to dine. He needed to be home. He passed John Mowbray, the Duke of Norfolk, returning home as he left the castle.

Elizabeth was pleased to see her husband return. He could see that she looked shaken and wondered what on earth William Catesby had wanted with his wife. He smiled reassuringly and took her hands. "At what does my lady want with Catesby? Do you have matters that require the legal mind?" He meant it kindly but was astounded when Elizabeth burst into tears. He gently led her to a nearby couch and, as she made herself comfortable, wiped a tear from her face.

"Eleanor gifted me, Fenny Compton, in early June." Her husband was somewhat perplexed. "And for that, you shed tears?" He gave a smile as he once again wiped her face. It was too much. His kindness, the loss of her sister, the terrible secret she had kept locked in her heart. In between sobs, she told him the story of Eleanor's secret marriage to King Edward. Her belief Eleanor had been murdered. The fear she felt was because she was virtually a witness to the wedding and had attended the dinner to celebrate the occasion. The duke was stunned. He sat there in silence for some time. Elizabeth had stopped crying. She looked at her husband's grave face and attempted to moisten her tongue, which had become quite dry.

The duke's thoughts returned to the memory of Eleanor's face when he had told them of the secret wedding of the king. He recalled her white face and the question. "Did the lady have a name?" He remembered her leaving the room in haste. He had thought it very strange at the time. Now he understood. Finally, he spoke in a broken voice. "The king has committed bigamy. His marriage is invalid, and his children bastards." It was beyond comprehension. Horrified, he recognised the danger of such knowledge. It would have been better not to know. He looked at his wife and saw the fear and sadness in her eyes. A sense of tenderness swept over him. He leaned forward, took her in his arms, and whispered. "My poor darling. And you have born this knowledge on your own all this time." He kissed the tears from her eyes. She relaxed and buried her head into his chest.

Chapter 8

Jacquetta received the news of the death of her husband Richard and their son John at her manor at Grafton Regis. Thomas Wake, a burly, roughly spoken retainer of Warwick, displayed no sympathy but wore a smirk as he provided details she didn't want to hear. Lord Rivers and their son were arrested in the Forest of Dean. Both were beheaded at Kenilworth at the command of the Duke of Clarence and Earl of Warwick. Jacquetta made no response. With eyes of steel, she stared into his. *The eyes are the windows of the soul.* Where had he heard those words?

He started to fidget uncomfortably at the prolonged silence. The roots of his hair tingled as fear crept up the nape of his neck. Warwick had sent him to accuse Jacquetta of witchcraft. He had been given the evidence for the trial. He was scared. Whose vengeance would be worse? The Earl of Warwick's if he failed to carry out the task or that of this witch if he succeeded?

He called to a group of men who were with him. "Arrest her!" He spat the words. "She will be tried here for witchcraft." Jacquetta gave a half smile. He was scared; he didn't dare touch her.

Wake had believed Jacquetta would be vulnerable and easily defeated now that her husband and oldest son were dead, King Edward, a prisoner of Warwick, and her younger son Anthony in London. He was confident the verdict would be guilty as charged, unless she resorted to witchcraft. He had not considered her power as a mother to the Queen of England and certainly not her astuteness.

Jacquetta was no fool. Warwick was a dangerous man, and she needed to remove the power from him. She made no objection Wake had ordered the trial to be at her manor. As soon as Wake left, leaving her under guard, she ordered a trusted servant to hastily take a message to the mayor and alderman of London asking them to investigate the claims. She had adroitly placed the authority in their hands. It was a strategy to get her more time.

The result was a fiasco.

Wake had claimed he found the effigies bound together in the keeping of the nunnery of Sewardsley, just five miles from

Grafton. He argued that John Daunger, a parish clerk, could verify how the Duchess of Bedford had left the effigies there. However, when summoned, Daunger panicked, and became reluctant to talk. He said he hadn't realised it was Countess Rivers they wanted him to lie about. It was too dangerous. The investigation negated the trial. For the time at least, Jacquetta was safe.

Thomas Wake, furious Jacquetta had outwitted him, contended it was sorcery that had saved her. Over a jug of ale, he spluttered to all who would listen. "She put a spell on Daunger so he would not testify. She resorted to sorcery on Sir Humphrey Neville, so he stirred up trouble and prevented Warwick from raising sufficient troops to quell it. As a consequence, Warwick was forced to allow Edward to appear in public in York to rally troops." He took a long gulp of his ale. He continued.

"She's a sorceress, alright. It was her as used magic to convince the guards to release the king so he could defeat Humphries. 'Ow, else would it 'ave happened? And why? So she could save her skin. No one dared touch her once Edward marched into London with the Dukes of Gloucester and Suffolk and a thousand men. Humphrey's lost his head, so he couldn't tell 'em he was bewitched." There was laughter. Wake shrugged his shoulders. "The king will pardon them, more fool him." He slammed his jug on the table.

"Warwick and the Duke of Clarence aren't to be trusted."

Heads turned at the remark made quietly by a man who had been listening to the conversation. "The King made a fool of Warwick by his secret marriage to Elizabeth Woodville while Warwick was arranging a foreign alliance. Warwick will never forgive him for that. He is planning to put Clarence on the throne. You wait and see. Edward needs to be less forgiving and watch his back." He stood and slowly made his way to the door, shaking his head as he walked.

The unknown man was Walter Hungerford. He delighted in frequenting places of gossip, amazed by how accurate news spread among the populace. Another source of information was at private gatherings the rich held. William Collingbourne, keeper of Ludgershall Castle, enjoyed such gatherings. How honoured he had felt that Edward granted him keeper for life of this beautiful castle where once kings hunted and enjoyed banquets.

He remembered his first visit. The castle stood proudly on the hill. Greystones glistened on the tall square turret as they caught the sunlight. He had watched the smoke from several chimneys as it swirled into the cool air, rising and disappearing as wisps into the sky. The aroma of rain and wood delighted his nostrils as he walked through damp forests, his feet crunching the fallen leaves and, afterward, the warmth of a roaring fire. On other occasions, he had watched the heavy doors under the stone archway slowly open as he sat on his magnificent chestnut horse, trotting under the avenue of huge oak trees, fascinated by the dappled light and then the rush forward as he gave his horse permission to fly.

William had a few guests staying at the castle. Walter and his wife, Henry Stafford, and his wife Margaret, Countess of Richmond. Lord Brownbridge and his wife, Lady Anne. Only Collingbourne was a bachelor. That was to change later in the year. Edward had harassed him for months to find a suitable wife. He had introduced him to many ladies of good breeding, but Collingbourne was disinclined to consider any of them. Edward chastised him. He knew the reason for Collingbourne's reluctance.

"It's no use you following her with your tongue hanging, William. She's taken. You require a wife. You need an heir, man. Get yourself a wife. You can still have your fun if you're smart enough. On my oath, it isn't hard to persuade a lady to your bedchamber if you have a mind to.

It wasn't only the king who urged him to get on with his life. Walter Hungerford, his dear friend, took delight in making little jibes about his attraction to Margaret, the Countess of Richmond. He recalled not long ago when he was entertaining a group of friends; he had felt particularly downhearted as he watched Margaret enter the room leaning on the arm of her husband. He had felt a piercing stab of jealousy. Walter had noticed his sour face. "Disappointed she's with her husband tonight?" He meant to snap his friend out of it, but Collingbourne had felt a wave of irritation. He took an inward breath before he spoke. "It's just a marriage of convenience." His words were cold.

"Convenient to whom?" Walter chortled. "It certainly is not convenient for you."

Collingbourne had finally chosen his lady. Just a few weeks ago, the King had slapped him on the back and beaming cried, "I've found a Margaret of your very own William. Margaret Pykering, heiress of St. John Norwood. She's the wealthy widow of Sir John Pykering. A proven mare, presented Sir John with two sons, so you shouldn't have any trouble getting yourself an heir." He gave Collingbourne a nudge and a wink. "That's if you are up to it, William." Collingbourne grinned. "I doubt if I could serve a dam as well as you, your majesty." Edward roared with laughter. "You are probably right there, William. Not many have my prowess. Nevertheless, it is our desire that you take this woman as your wife. I've even decided to give you a wedding present of Bradfield Manor to start your married life." Collingbourne was about to remind Edward he had Ludgershall Castle, but Edward anticipated his words. "Keep that for your fun," he whispered the words as he swept out of the room.

Collingbourne's thoughts were interrupted by the heated discussion in which Walter and Henry Stafford were engaged.

"The king is a fool to trust George and Warwick again." Walter frowned as he spoke. "They'll not be satisfied with his generosity."

There was a nod of approval.

"The trouble is," Margaret ventured, "Clarence doesn't believe his brother has a right to the crown, particularly since the rumours about his illegitimacy."

"But who in their right mind believes that!" William snorted. Margaret gave a slight smile but said no more. She began fingering her bracelet, lost in her own thoughts. Henry Stafford watched his wife as she sat there. He knew her loyalty was not to Edward but believed she was doing her best to accept the new king. She constantly had her son Henry Tudor on her mind. It was her plan to get him a place in court. The Woodville's were Lancastrians at heart, but they had changed their support to the Yorkists since Elizabeth became queen. Couldn't her son be trusted to do the same? Couldn't he become a favourite of Edward? How dearly she would love to have him at court. She had shown her loyalty by serving Queen Elizabeth. Stafford loved his wife but was never quite sure where he stood with her. If it became a choice between him and her son, he was not convinced she would put him before Henry Tudor. But he wasn't even sure about himself. Would he put Henry Tudor before Edward if it came to the crunch?

Stafford knew Warwick and Clarence were not to be trusted. He had heard that they were deliberately circulating rumours that Edward's claim he was going to deal with Wells was a lie. It was rumoured that he was going to punish those who were involved in the previous uprising that resulted in his imprisonment. He had also heard that Edward had summoned Warwick and Clarence to meet him at Fotheringham, but his informers had told him they had no intention of going. Edward believed they would support him.

He had not admitted any of this to Margaret. It would raise her hopes that Edward would lose his crown, and if he did, it might not be Clarence who would wear it next. Elizabeth had not given him a son, but she was pregnant again. Margaret lived in eternal hope. She sincerely believed her son Henry would be crowned king. She just had to be patient.

About halfway through supper, Sir John Cheney arrived. Collingbourne rose from the table and offered him a seat. He sat, looking longingly at the cold meats heaped onto his plate.

"We thought you weren't going to make it." Hungerford laughed as he watched Cheney tuck in. Cheney, mouth full, began to speak.

"There's more trouble. Wells was defeated, and they took his casket. Oh, my Lord! What evidence of treason against the king they discovered? He pronged two pieces of meat, cramming them in his mouth as he spoke. "And they found incriminating letters pushed in a helmet. They took Wells and his friends to King Edward at Grantham. It didn't take long for them to confess Warwick and Clarence were in it deep. Wells admitted the plan was to get rid of Edward and then make Clarence King.

Collingbourne sat back at the table. "Thank God Edward has discovered it. He can't let them get away with it this time. They have gone too far.

"They know that," Cheney slowed down his eating. "Edward is furious, and rightly so. He's declared them as traitors. They are on the run. Edward thinks they will go to sea. He's already instructed Lord Wenlock in Calais to refuse the traitors to land."

Margaret, the Countess of Richmond, sat and listened with interest. Edward did not seem to be sitting on his throne very securely these days. Perhaps it was time to assist with a slight push and make room for Henry. But no! Clarence was still in the running. It had to be admitted that Clarence was living dangerously. Edward would surely lose patience before long. It was not Henry's time yet, but she must alert Jasper to be ready.

A few weeks later, rumours began that the traitors had finally shown their hand and changed allegiances. Warwick had received a shocking blow from the gods. Wild storms at sea, and Lord Wenlock's refusal to allow them to land at Calais, contributed to the loss of his expected heir. Isabella delivered her son, but the labour was too long, and she couldn't receive the help she needed; Clarence's heir went straight to heaven. Warwick refused to take responsibility. The blame was Edward's. If he hadn't commanded that they were not to be given permission to land at Calais, all would have been well. His anger became an obsession. He was determined to get rid of Edward for good. Without thinking of Clarence and Isabella, he decided to change plans. He had another daughter, didn't he? Anne. What if he, the kingmaker, arranged for her to marry Henry's son, Prince Edward, and he became a Lancastrian King of England? The result would be the same, his daughter would be the Queen of England, and he would be rid of the ungrateful York king.

King Edward stood dumbfounded. Elizabeth had just informed him that one of her ladies had received a message. It was from George, Duke of Clarence. His sister-in-law, Anne Neville, was to be married to Edward of Lancaster at Angers Cathedral in December.

Edward gritted his teeth. "That he could stoop so low."

"What does it mean?" Elizabeth was confused. She believed he was planning to get Clarence on the throne and that his daughter Isabella would be queen.

"Poor George." Edward's words were sincere. "It seems, Warwick had other plans that did not suit him. Hopefully, he has seen the light. We must encourage him to defy Warwick and inform us of the traitor's movements. Clearly, Warwick used his daughter to convince Margaret of Anjou he could be trusted to be loyal to her."

He strode to the door. Action is needed. "I will immediately send for Richard, Lord Hastings and your son Anthony. We need to prepare for an invasion. No doubt Louis will fund his cousin Margaret to fulfil her wish to restore Henry to the throne."

Richard was sitting in a chair mulling over what Edward had told him about George and Warwick's latest movements. Had Warwick gone mad throwing his lot in with Queen Margaret? The news that distressed him most was the marriage of Anne Neville to Prince Edward. What was Warwick thinking? He had grown up with Anne, and he was very fond of her. It saddened him she had been thrust among the Lancastrians. His thoughts turned to George. What did he think of the marriage? He gave a short cough, then addressed Edward.

"You would be well advised to ensure George chooses you over Warwick. "Richard had already proved himself on the battlefield. Edward admired this young man, his brother, who had been so loyal to him. He sighed. "So many chances I have given your brother; how can I be sure of his loyalty?" Richard frowned. It was true that George had been a consistent annoyance, always making wrong decisions, but he was sure his heart belonged to Edward rather than Warwick.

"Perhaps if you promised him a pardon, he would rally." Edward rolled his eyes. Richard twisted his lips in wry amusement as he acknowledged how preposterous his suggestion sounded. He was well aware Edward had been extraordinarily patient with George. There were those who accused him of weakness. But

Edward was definitely not weak. Warwick was dogmatic, and George easily influenced.

Edward sent George a message through the woman who attended to his wife. It was brief but sincere. 'My dear George, It is our wish you return to us. Do not consort with the Lancastrians. We are willing to offer you a free pardon.'

Richard had been right. George responded to the king's message quickly. He was furious with Warwick, who he felt had betrayed him. He would keep Edward informed of Warwick's movements and promised to defect to Edward's side when he returned to England. Edward was pleased but wondered how long it would take George to cause him grief again.

The queen was in her late weeks of pregnancy. She despaired when Edward told her of another rebellion in the north. He had to go to suppress it.

"My love, I have arranged with your mother that you both stay in the Tower for safety reasons. We will soon overpower Lord Fitzhugh, but we know Warwick is close to returning. I cannot concentrate on what I must do if you are in danger." Elizabeth, touched by his concern for her, was sure that she was carrying a son for him this time. It would be foolish to put him at risk. She thought of Isabel, who had lost her baby as a result of men at war. As much as she disliked Clarence, she felt deep sympathy for his wife. Edward was right. She could not endanger their son.

It happened so quickly. Edward received the news at York on 25th September that Warwick and Clarence had landed at Plymouth and Dartmouth on 13th September, nearly two weeks ago. He had an army of 2000 troops.

Edward was infuriated when the Earl of Northumberland ignored his urgent summons and turned his 6000 men against him. What was going on?

He had retired for the night when he awoke to Richard shaking him. His eyes widened when Richard urged him to rise immediately. "Don't tarry, Edward. Warwick is coming for you. We must go. We haven't a chance. Hastings and Anthony are mounted ready – come, we must flee!"

The journey was a nightmare. Edward feared they would not get through the waters at The Wash. It was a miracle no one was drowned. They made their way safely to Kings Lynn. How could they escape? The boatman's hand was out for money. They had no money. It had all happened without warning. Had Clarence been true to him?

The boatman eyed the luxurious coat on the king. Lined with fur! Good quality, too, if he was not mistaken. That would keep out the icy winds. He agreed to trade it for the price of escape. Relieved, they were on their way, Edward thought about Elizabeth. He had not had a chance to say goodbye. Thank God she had agreed to stay at the Tower. She would be safe there. He was wrong.

Elizabeth was distraught when she heard the news that Edward and her son had been forced to flee. Instinctively, she realised her danger. Henry was also in the Tower. They would be coming to release him and restore him to the throne. It was no longer safe. Jacquetta consoled her. "We will seek refuge in Westminster Abbey. We will go tonight. I will gather the children. We will be safe in the sanctuary." Elizabeth sent for the Abbot of Westminster. He agreed to give a message to the mayor that it was imperative she, the queen, surrender the Tower for her and her children's safety. Elizabeth was afraid. Would she ever see Edward again? Were her children safe? She buried her face in her hands, and her body shook as the sobs took over. Her daughter Elizabeth ran over and threw her arms around her. "Don't cry, mother. Our father will come and take us home. God will tell him he must."

Chapter 9

"You have to admit, King Henry has shown unprecedented kindness to Queen Elizabeth." Margaret, Countess of Richmond, spoke with pride. They were seated in the Great Room at Ludgershall Castle, discussing the plight of King Edward and Warwick's success in restoring the Lancastrian king to his throne.

Collingbourne was stretched in a chair, his long legs covered by jade tights. He wore a pair of quality leather boots. His arm hung over the side of the chair in a relaxed and lazy manner.

"Henry is just a puppet king," Collingbourne scoffed. "Warwick is pulling the strings."

"Are you sure? If that was so, isn't it surprising Elizabeth has been treated so well," Margaret crowed. "Don't you think it amazing that Warwick would give Queen Elizabeth such support to ensure her son was born safely? King Henry allowed John Gould, the butcher, to supply meat to her. She was allowed her own midwife, physician, and doctor. I would not have thought Warwick would have desired a safe birth for Edward's son and heir. Perhaps Warwick's power over Henry is not as great as you suggest." She lowered her eyes.

"Or maybe Warwick didn't care if Henry demonstrated kindness. Maybe Warwick is confident that Edward has lost his throne for good." Lord Cheney's tone was gruff. Sir Walter Hungerford nodding his head in agreement, added, "He doesn't see the new prince as a threat. His daughter, Anne's marriage to Henry's son, rather secures the throne.

"You surely agree that Henry's proclamation forbidding any man on pain of death to 'defoul or distrouble' the church or sanctuaries or anyone in them was a deliberate move to protect the queen and her family. Surely he deserves praise for that?" Margaret was determined to show the Lancastrian king in a favourable light. She sought support for her own son, Henry. She wanted to shout the news that Jasper had returned to England with the Earl of Warwick. She wanted to scream to the world, Jasper had taken her son to King Henry who predicted that one day, he would wear a crown. But she dared not. Her husband was scowling at her from across the room. It was too soon. As if he knew what she was thinking, Collingbourne sat up straight and spoke directly to her.

"You don't think Edward will stay away for long, do you? Edward will return. Then he'll get rid of Henry once and for all."

The countess pouted. There was a great deal of truth in what Collingbourne said. King Henry was weak, and no one knew when he would have another bout of madness. She must tread carefully. It would not do to lose her place at court if, indeed, Edward did return.

Collingbourne was right. Edward was not away for long. Margaret of York, Edward's sister, persuaded her husband Charles to meet Edward for talks. They met in early January. Edward was a guest of Jacquetta's brother, Jacques of Luxembourg. Charles agreed to help his brother-in-law and support the Yorkist dynasty. Within six months, Edward's ships could be sighted from the coast of Norfolk. It was a daring venture. The Duke of Clarence had kept his promise, and was in touch.

Despite his difficulty in persuading Hull and Beverley to allow him entrance to York, Edward succeeded by concealing his true purpose. Edward declared his loyalty to Henry VI and wore the livery of the ostrich-feather badge pledging allegiance to Edward, Prince of Wales. He claimed he had come to repossess his Duchy of York. He marched forward to Coventry, where George had informed him Warwick was waiting in the castle for reinforcements. George had sent a letter to Warwick not to fight Edward until he arrived to support him. George, at last, achieved revenge on Warwick. He ignored his father-in-law and gave his support to his brother King Edward as he had promised.

Queen Elizabeth could not believe her eyes when Edward entered her place of sanctuary.

Princess Elizabeth, upon seeing her father, squealed with delight. "You see, mother. I told you God would tell father he must come to us." Edward held his son in his arms for the first time. Bright blue eyes steadfastly stared up at him. For a brief second, Edward wondered if Eleanor's son had such blue eyes. A flash of guilt brought tear to his own. Elizabeth watched him, believing her husband showed tears of joy. They were not; they were tears of sorrow that he had never looked into the eyes of his true heir. But there was joy in his heart, also. Eleanor's words simply overshadowed it. "You will never have a son on the throne, Edward." What did the future hold for this child? He pushed such thoughts out of his mind.

News reached Collingbourne that King Edward, the Dukes of Gloucester, and Clarence, William, and Lord Hastings were victorious at the Battle of Barnet in spite of being outnumbered by Warwick's forces. The gods must have been on Edward's side because Oxford's livery badge of the sun with rays was confused in the mist for Edward's sun in splendour. Warwick's troops turned on themselves. Warwick, who had witnessed the death of his brother, admitted defeat. Walter Hungerford was with Collingbourne when the news arrived. Collingbourne spoke in a tone of satisfaction.

"The latest news is Warwick is dead. Edward had given orders he wanted him taken alive—my oath. I can't think why. The man was a traitor. But either by defiance or accident, he was killed."

Walter nodded. "It is his conscience, no doubt. He owed Warwick his crown. One could argue Edward betrayed him; Warwick simply retaliated." Collingbourne frowned. "Our King has shown no mercy to those who crossed him. He is determined to rid England of the Lancastrians for good. I guarantee King Henry will no longer be allowed to live. Edward has procrastinated too long." Walter ran his tongue over his teeth, then spoke. "What is amazing, young George turned up to support Edward. But so many betrayals. How can Edward trust him?" Collingbourne stood up to stretch his legs as he thought about Walter's words. "I guess he wasn't too happy about Warwick's change of plans. He thought the crown was for him and Isabella; instead, Warwick offered his younger daughter Anne as a wife for Margaret's son Edward. He would still have a daughter on the throne. Too bad about Isabel and George." He poured some wine into a goblet and offered it to Walter, who gladly stretched an arm to take it. He poured another, then returned to his chair and spoke almost to himself. It's frightening how Clarence could be a friend, brother, and ally to Prince Edward and then, totally ignoring pleas for mercy, run a sword through his heart." He shook his head at the very thought. Walter raised his goblet. "That's the madness of war, my friend."

Shortly after the death of Warwick, Margaret, Countess of Richmond, called on Collingbourne. Their relationship had strengthened. Margaret felt she had an ally in Collingbourne. She had secret hopes that she could change his allegiance from Edward and instead support her son.

He could sense there was something wrong as soon as she entered the room. Smudges of red around her eyes contrasted with the paleness of her face. She was pleased Collingbourne was alone. She sat on the chair he offered, but no sooner than he was seated, she rose and began pacing the room. He stood immediately and watched as her face distorted and she burst into tears. Without thinking, Collingbourne stepped forward and put an arm around her shoulder. He hated seeing her so distressed. He knew her husband, Henry Stafford, had been badly wounded during the Battle of Barnet. Perhaps her tears were for him. He hated himself for the stab of jealousy that caused him to flinch.

"Is Henry worse?" His concern was genuine. She shook her head. "Henry is in constant pain. His doctor applies leeches several times a week on his wounds, but I fear they are slow to heal. I pray for him daily and thank the Lord his life was not taken." Her bottom lip began to tremble. "Then what ails you, Margaret? " He wanted to take the pain from her face.

"My son. He is only fourteen. He is defenceless against Edward. His life is in danger." She brushed a hand across her face. Collingbourne felt a tenderness that he had never felt before.

"What can you do?" He spoke, stroking back a lock of hair that had escaped from her headdress.

She stepped back from his embrace. "Jasper must take him out of the country," she whispered as if the walls had ears. "Both he and Henry are included in the Act of Attainder that has been passed against the leading Lancastrians. I can trust Jasper to take care of him as if he was his own son – in fact, he has promised me he will do so." The tears had stopped.

"You must keep in favour with Edward, dearest." The word of endearment slipped out. She made no audible comment but was pleased and stored it away.

"I intend to, Will." She smiled at him. There was a slight familiarity with the abbreviated version of his name. He liked it. She knew he did. She was well aware of her growing power over him. It was slowly developing, but she would feed it and water it. Margaret had learned it was important to have power over men. It was essential if she was to achieve her dream. She needed to gather as many hearts as possible for her cause.

Collingbourne was flattered she had come to him with her sorrow. He took her hand and was genuine in his offer of help. She raised an eye. Was it too soon to tell him that he could? He had the ear of the king. He could persuade Edward to allow her son Henry to stay, to pardon him, and reverse his attainder. But if that should fail? Yes, it was too soon. She would abide by her time. There would be a time when Collingbourne's connection with the king and his family would serve her well.

In less than four months, Henry Stafford lost the fight for his life. Margaret's prayers had been answered, and her husband no longer suffered the agonising pain he had been born for six months after he was wounded at Barnet.

Collingbourne was surprised when Margaret told him she was marrying Thomas Stanley so soon after her husband's death.

"But why? Why are you marrying this man? You can't be in love with him." They were walking in Margaret's rose garden at Lydiad and had just reached the centre. Margaret bent forward and selected a magnificent red bloom. She snapped it from the bush, breathed in the delightful perfume then offered it to him. "Here, Will. A token of my love for you." He tightened his lips. She was playing with him. She knew how he felt about her. She observed his effort to control his anger. Men. You could read them like a book. She leaned forward, kissed him lightly on the lips, and whispered. "It will make no difference to our relationship, Will, my dear. It is simply a marriage of convenience."

"Does he know that?" His voice was terse.

"Of course. It will not do for a woman in my position to be widowed for long. The king expects me to marry. In the past, a husband was found for me. It was never a question of love, as you know well. Now, I am in the position to choose whom I wish." Collingbourne mumbled. "Why not wish to marry me?" She slapped his hand with the rose that she was still holding. "I wish to marry Stanley because he is steward to King Edward, and it will necessitate me living at court." Collingbourne couldn't help laughing at her blatant honesty. She sat on an elaborately carved garden seat, patting the bench and inviting him to sit with her. "You see a marriage of convenience. Since I will no longer have a need for this manor, and you are so much in love with it, I intend that this should become your seat. Naturally, I will have reasons to visit on occasion." He sat beside her and lifted her hand to his lips.

"You are a calculating minx. And why do you wish to be at court rather than spend your days in this beautiful environment, or need I ask? You are scheming to get your son there, and I know you, it will not be as a subject but as King of England." She smiled. "Are you talking treason, my love?"

It had been Collingbourne's dearest wish to marry Margaret Beaufort, Countess of Richmond, but he was well aware that the king did not consider it a suitable match. Edward had decided that

Margaret Pykering, the daughter and heiress of Sir John Norwood, should be William's bride. She was the widow of Sir James Pykering and came with a large fortune. In the spring of 1474, William married Margaret in a pretty little church in Wiltshire. The bride was petite and attractive. She wore a beautiful rose-pink silk gown. Hair, the colour of ebony, was almost covered with an elaborately embroidered headdress. In her hands, she carried a white leather-covered prayer book.

The king was well pleased. William had already amassed land in Wiltshire and London and had become a very powerful man serving as commissioner and Sheriff of Wiltshire shortly after his marriage. The king had honoured him. Life was great. He was successful, powerful, and extremely rich. Best of all, his Wiltshire seat, Lydiard was held by Margaret Beaufort, the love of his life who had kept her word and offered it to him after her marriage. The great house was one of his favourite and had become his seat since 1472. The building itself was long and rectangular but with Gothic arches made from cream stone. The ceilings were high, and the great room doors opened out to patios filled with roses.

The gardens were spectacular and boasted oaks, beech, and horse chestnut that were many years old and spread their huge branches wide, casting shade in the heat of summer and providing magnificent autumn colour. How he enjoyed his walks, the leaves crunching under his feet as winter approached. Walks and tumbles into the sweet musky smell of a leaf pile with Margaret, his love. Treasured memories.

Chapter 10

King Edward was strolling alone through his forest at Ludgershall Park. He needed to get away from his court and remove himself from his queen. Although undoubtedly warranted, her constant complaints about his brother George drove him to distraction. Yes, it was true George was a thorn in his side. He was guilty of conspiring against Elizabeth and her family, himself included. He reminded himself that his young brothers were his responsibility after their father was killed. He was only 18 himself. The first thing he did when he became king was to bring them both home from Burgundy for his coronation. He had been generous. They both had dukedoms within weeks of arriving in England. He sighed. He didn't have this problem with Richard. He had proved himself on the battlefield. He was loyal. It was sometimes difficult to remember he was still so young. But George... Edward closed his eyes. His patience had snapped when he heard that George was spreading the word that Edward was a bastard and not fit to be king. The Queen had lost all sense of decorum and screamed, "The Tower! Lock him in the Tower, and don't let him out!" There was no controlling her. Her ladies tried their best. He had swept out of the room. His anger consumed him. He didn't need a woman to tell him what to do. He wished he could lock her in the Tower with George. The thought amused him. Perhaps that would be the worst punishment of all.

He breathed in the delightful aroma of the forest as he walked under the mighty oaks. It was a warm autumn day, and the leaves were beginning to turn. A red squirrel was nibbling an acorn. It looked up as it heard the crunch of the undergrowth, but it continued eating. His thoughts returned to George. He recalled their last meeting. George showed no repentance. Edward looked around the room. His brother had nothing to complain about. The furnishings were suitable for a nobleman's home. It was hardly a prison.

"How many times do you expect me to pardon you?" George rolled his eyes. He was dressed in the latest fashion. Edward noted the particoloured hose. Edward tried again. "Why, George, why do you break your promise to behave?"

George leaned back in his chair, stretching a leg to display his fashionable hose. Then as if to antagonize his brother, he drawled, "So you have sent Stillington to keep me informed." His eyes spoke more than words. It was true he had sent Stillington to the Tower. He had heard rumours. Stillington was still angry that Edward had replaced him as chancellor a few years back. There was talk of revenge. Would he dare to speak now? God's truth. After the power and money that had been bestowed on him, would he dare to break the silence? A couple of young deer rushed through the forest, jolting Edward's thoughts back to the present. A good hunt would be invigorating! He must instruct Collingbourne to arrange it.

Queen Elizabeth was angry that her husband had not made a decision about George. He had to go. She had never forgiven or forgotten that he, with Warwick, was guilty of the beheading of her dear father and brother. Time had passed, but she would never forget. Yet Edward repeatedly pardoned his wayward brother. This time though, this time he would not get away with his treason. She was certain he had knowledge of Edward's bigamy. Edward suspected Stillingham had talked. He had sent him to the Tower as a warning but had no evidence. She had heard another rumour. That wretched Duchess of Norfolk had berated her husband in the hearing of one of her ladies for telling Clarence that Edward was not all that he appeared to be. They had been enjoying several jugs of ale, and Clarence had been complaining that Edward had once again stood in his way of a perfect marriage. After the death of his wife Isabel, his sister, Margaret, Duchess of Burgundy, had suggested that Mary, her stepdaughter, would be a good match for brother Clarence. Edward opposed the marriage. With no explanation why, he declared it was not a suitable match. Clarence complained bitterly to John, the Duke of Norfolk. The injustice of it all! John had laughed and patted Clarence on the back and spoken jovially. "Have another secret wedding, my man. It succeeded last time with Isabel. You got away with that. Why, God's Oath, Edward managed two of them himself, didn't he? It seems to be a family trait." Clarence picked up his ears. He had heard a rumour of the kind from Stillington, but when questioned, the Bishop denied it. He questioned his friend John further, but no sooner had the words left the Duke's lips; he realised his error and refused to make another comment, changing the topic to a prospective hunt they had planned. Clarence stored the comment away.

Elizabeth, Duchess of Norfolk, knelt beside her sister Eleanor's tomb. She could not visit as often as she wished but always made an effort three or four times a year. Today she had extra special news, but first, she spoke to Eleanor about her secret son. She hoped so much that Eleanor could hear her, and although it had been many years since Eleanor had died, Elizabeth had kept her promise. She would visit and care for him. "He is growing so tall," she laughed. "And he can read both Latin and English already. He is a very happy boy, and has made a new friend called Anthony. He tells me he is soon to work with Francis, an elderly monk who will teach him herb lore. You would be so proud of him.

I also have some wonderful news. Do you remember I told you I appealed to Our Lady of Walsingham once more? My appeal was successful. John and I are expecting a child again. Naturally, we both pray for a son. We have been blessed with our sweet, adorable daughter Anne. We are grateful, of course. John will join me this Christmas in Norwich, then will return to Framlingham Castle, where he is in so much demand. I have been instructed to stay in Norwich and rest.

Queen Elizabeth, still angry that Edward had done nothing but sent George, Duke of Clarence, to the Tower, discussed the matter with Jacquetta. "I will insist that Edward put's George away for good. Jaquetta frowned at her daughter. She could feel trouble brewing. Her daughter appeared constantly angry. Was it fear? Elizabeth raised her voice. "Mother, are you listening to me at all?" Jacquetta touched her daughter's hand in an attempt to calm her.

Elizabeth leaned closer to her mother. "I believe the Duke of Norfolk knows about Edward's marriage to that woman. I have a plan." Jacquetta raised her eyebrows. Elizabeth leaned forward and lowered her voice. "The Duke of Norfolk has enormous wealth but no male heir. But he does have a daughter, Lady Anne de Mowbray. She is very young, but that is of no consequence. I will suggest that Edward arrange a marriage between Lady Anne and our younger son Richard Duke of York. An excellent match, don't you think? What wealth will come with the young bride! Of course, the marriage contract will include a clause to ensure the wealth and extensive lands will pass to Richard even in the case of Anne's death. Elizabeth glowed with excitement.

Jacquetta agreed it would be an excellent match, but... Elizabeth scowled. "But?" But what? Her voice was icy. Jaquetta sensed Elizabeth's rising anger. She spoke her thoughts. "The duke is still young himself, and I hear the Duchess has appealed to our Lady of Walsingham. She could have a son yet." Elizabeth applied a false smile and spoke testily. "True, my mother dear, but John de Mowbray, the extremely wealthy Duke of Norfolk, knows a secret that could well shorten his life considerably." Jacquetta frowned. "How much her daughter had changed! Once, she was sweet and loving. She would never have thought of such a thing."

Whether it was his own idea or one that had been planted in his head by his wife, King Edward was not really sure. He had grown to like the prospect of a union between his younger son Richard and the infant Lady Anne de Mowbray. He tried to convince himself that it was for Eleanor he had agreed to the marriage. Lady

Anne was, after all, her niece. She had been honoured by the King of England. But he knew Eleanor would not have been fooled. She would have been well aware that the enormous wealth young Anne would bring as a bride would have been foremost in his thinking. He dismissed Eleanor from his thoughts. He decided to visit John de Mowbray and make arrangements for the betrothal. It would be better to go directly to Framlingham Castle. His informants had told him that Elizabeth, Duchess of Norfolk, would not be with her husband, for she had been instructed to rest. What better time to visit? He always felt uncomfortable in the presence of Elizabeth. She never said anything inappropriate, but her looks were enough. Her eyes sought his soul. They accused him of her sister's death. She had knowledge of his marriage to Eleanor. He needed to keep her silent, and although he hadn't verbally threatened her, the pardon he had given was deliberately ambiguous, but she knew it was a warning.

King Edward arrived at Framlingham Castle on 30th December 1476 with a small retinue. Although given little warning, the Duke was there to greet him. Edward sprung from his horse and strode forward, waving his hand dismissively as men bowed and women curtseyed. Edward reached his host, who bowed before him.

"My apologies for such little warning Norfolk, but I have important business to discuss with you. Shall we go inside? Norfolk led the way. He turned, pleased at the initiative of his men servants. They had already relieved the king's retinue of their mounts and were showing the way to refreshment.

The King had waved all his companions away. Norfolk apologized for Elizabeth's absence. "No need. No need." Edward sunk into a huge chair full of cushions. He sighed with satisfaction as he leaned back, enjoying the comfort. He spoke to Norfolk standing before him, head bowed. "Be seated, man. We want no formality." Norfolk acquiesced. What in God's name was the reason for this visit? Had Edward discovered that he knew about his bigamy? Had Clarence been fool enough to tell him? He had not said another word since that dreadful night. The duke felt a little knot of fear begin to uncurl in his stomach. Nothing prepared him for the words he was hearing. "We have come to discuss a betrothal of your daughter Lady Anne to our son, Richard, Duke of York." There, it was said.

Norfolk stared into space. His baby daughter, and marriage. It didn't seem conceivable. He knew it was the custom in noble households to arrange such marriages between young sons and daughters, but Anne was still a baby.

Edward looked at him impatiently. What was wrong with the man? Here stood the King of England making this magnificent offer, an offer the envy of many, and all he could do was stare like a dalcop. He stood up and began walking around the room, clicking his fingers. Anyone who knew the king was aware this was not a good sign.

"The Pope would not like it." Norfolk had spoken at last. Edward stopped walking and scowled. 'We will get a special dispensation. God's Oath man. Is that your only problem?" He gave a dry laugh and sat again. He had expected Norfolk to accept his offer without hesitation.

Norfolk had his own thoughts. What would Elizabeth think of such a marriage to the son of a man who had treated her sister so badly? He could not make such a commitment without talking to his wife. He knew though he need take care not to offend the king. He smiled. There was no need to make a decision until he had talked to Elizabeth. She was cool-headed. She would have the answer.

"Your majesty, I am honoured you have asked for the hand of my daughter Lady Anne on behalf of your son. This is, as I am sure you will agree, a matter in all courtesy that I must discuss with Elizabeth, the Duchess." Edward thought about his own Elizabeth. Yes, she would be angry if he didn't consult her on such matters, but also angry that Norfolk hadn't immediately accepted with gratitude the honour of marriage of his daughter to their son. He gave a little laugh. There was no getting away from it; Elizabeth gets angry about so many things these days. He stood and made as if to leave but paused as the aroma of food wafted through the air. He hadn't realised how hungry he was. He gladly accepted the

Duke's offer of dinner. His mood changed in anticipation of delight as he moved towards the delicious fragrances of juices from cooked meats and sauces.

The King was in good humour throughout the dinner. The meal was delicious, and the ale even better. He had a positive feeling about the proposed union of Lady Anne as his daughter-in-law. Only a fool would refuse. Besides, there were ways and means to achieve what one desires. Once he decided to leave, he made a quick farewell to his host. His parting words were, "May Elizabeth deliver you a son Norfolk." He laughed, "Don't give up if she doesn't; you might have to wait until Lady Anne delivers you a grandson." He strode out of the room, his retinue struggling to keep up.

Two weeks later, the shocking news reached Elizabeth that her husband had died at Framlingham Castle. She collapsed. He was only 31 years old, and had shown no health issues.

The doctors did not know the cause of the Duke's death, but suggested it could have been his heart. His steward had found him on the floor of the Great Room, in the early hours of the morning. His death was a mystery. His steward said he had spent the evening entertaining visitors, who were unknown to the steward. He had believed they were to stay the night, The Duke had dismissed him as the hour was late. Concerned that the duke had not retired for the night he had checked to see if the duke needed anything, and that is when he discovered him, on the floor. He was not breathing. There was no sign of the visitor, and in fact they had not stayed as expected.

For days Elizabeth took to her bed. At first, she did not want to live, but one night Eleanor came to her. She watched as her sister moved closer and enfolded her in her arms just as she used to do when they were little. She was in a place of serene peace. Then Eleanor spoke quietly. "You must struggle on, dearest; your little daughter needs you as does my son. You have another child in your womb. Don't give up, darling heart. It isn't your time yet. You have much to do. She felt her sister's kisses on her eyes. Be brave, my little sister. I am always with you. The vision disappeared, but Elizabeth smiled. Eleanor was with her. She wasn't alone. She could sense her spirit around her. It would be difficult, she knew, but Eleanor was right. She would manage whatever lay in her path.

Elizabeth was not really surprised when the child she was carrying entered the world long before he was due. He was stillborn. The stress of unexpectedly losing John, her husband, must have contributed to her baby's death. John de Mowbray had been laid to rest in a newly made tomb at Thetford Priory.

She did not know King Edward had approached her late husband about the marriage of his son to her daughter until weeks later when Edward called on her.

He sympathized the loss of the duke, her husband. He told her that her husband was keen on the union of his son Richard, and Lady Anne. He added, although the duke hadn't wished to agree to the arrangement until he had spoken to her, he, the King, was confident it was his wish. Elizabeth naturally desired to support her husband's wishes but refused to be rushed. The loss of her baby shattered all hope. She hated the thought of losing her little girl too. Once married, although still a child, she would be expected to live with her new family. That was the way of things. She remembered how disappointed she had been when Eleanor had married and gone to live in a castle, how she missed her. It was also true that she hated King Edward for the way he had treated her sister. He had taken Eleanor away from her, and even if he didn't murder her himself, he was responsible. But Eleanor had loved him.

Many nights she lay awake wondering what to do. It couldn't be denied the marriage had many benefits for her little girl. She prayed for guidance. She didn't want to give up her daughter so soon. She asked Eleanor, but the room remained silent. Her mind was made up a few months later when Anne ran into the room laughing. She stopped suddenly. "Where is Papa? I want Papa to play." Elizabeth realised how lonely it must be for her little daughter. The house was so quiet. She had been so miserable with self-pity. Her daughter needed more. Her decision made; she contacted Edward and told him to proceed with arrangements for the marriage.

She watched her little daughter with pride. She wore a beautiful velvet gown and a small golden coronet on her head and was escorted by Richard, Duke of Gloucester; she walked into St. Stephen's Chapel, head held high, to join the royal family all waiting under a canopy of gold cloth. Once the ceremony was over, Elizabeth was convinced she had made the correct decision. Princess Anne was surrounded by the noblest families of the land and now was truly one of them.

Chapter 11

Richard, Duke of Gloucester, stroked the feather of his quill across his lips. He was listening to yet another list of complaints of high treason committed by his brother, the Duke of Clarence, against King Edward. He couldn't believe George could be such a fool. Edward himself chaired this meeting. Anthony Woodville, the queen's brother, was speaking. "Her majesty is incensed about the insults about her family she had received. The Duke of Clarence has even gone as far as to say she is not the legitimate wife of Edward." He put his hand to his forehead as if suffering from a terrible headache. Richard spoke. "Would you agree your sister has a great dislike for George? " Woodville looked sharply across the room to Richard. Where was such a question coming from? He frowned, but reluctantly agreed.

"Perhaps that is true, Your Grace, particularly since George, with Warwick, was responsible for the removal of the heads of the bodies of her husband and eldest son." Walter Hungerford noted the slight amusement on Collingbourne's face at Woodville's response. Woodville continued. "The thing is, George has been pardoned so many times and then simply offends again. It is a poor example to others who are whispering behind doors that Edward is weak as far as his brother is concerned." There was silence, but all knew Woodville had spoken the truth.

Edward watched and listened. He would agree he had been soft on George and probably would have continued to be if it hadn't been for the fear that George might have been made aware of his relationship with Eleanor. If he let George on the loose again, it might be his own undoing. He had to be silenced. The Queen was not going to stand any more. He knew from experience she and her mother would stop at nothing to protect the validity of her marriage. He had been surprised at her reaction to John de Mowbray's death. There was no pity, just a comment that made him alert. "He should have learnt to hold his tongue." If she suspected for one moment that George also knew the secret, she would show no mercy. But what if George talked before she had a chance to silence him too? It was too much of a risk. He must steer the thinking of this meeting to see George had played his last card.

"My Lords," the King broke the silence. "Our patience with the Duke of Clarence has been born by consideration of his youth. We love our brother George, but that love has not been reciprocated. We call to remembrance the many great conspiracies, malicious and heinous treason of which he has been guilty. We forgave and welcomed him into our arms. However, it has come to our knowledge that he has conspired a much more malicious, unnatural, and loathsome treason against us. Specifically, Clarence has published and said falsely that the king, our sovereign lord, was a bastard and not born to reign over us. This plotting against his family and king, who has always been generous, bestowing gifts and honours on him, is unnatural. We are also informed that Clarence obtained and got an exemplification under the great seal of Henry VI. It expressively states that 'if his son Edward died without an heir, he, the Duke of Clarence and his heirs should be kings of this land.' We are profoundly disappointed that George, Duke of Clarence, conspired with King Henry to take our crown and that George, our brother, has kept this secret from us. In view of the serious nature of these crimes, we ask for your advice and judgement on our brother, George, Duke of Clarence."

Little more needed to be said. It was unanimously agreed that George, Duke of Clarence, be convicted and attained of high treason. King Edward allowed no visitors before his brother's execution; only he himself visited him.

George was calmly stretched out on a couch. He was still elegantly dressed and showed no distress about the verdict. He did not rise when the King entered. Edward ignored the deliberate insolence.

"My dear George, it grieves me that it has come to this. This time you really went too far. You gave me little choice but to present your case for judgement."

George smiled. "Ah, my brother the King. And what I wonder would be the verdict of your trial? How would the people judge you? But your day of judgement will come. "

Edward ignored the comment. He knew George was taunting him but wasn't sure if he was referring to his marriage to Eleanor. "I've come to ask you the manner of your execution. Do you have a preference?"

George roared with laughter. 'How so very kind. Would I like the sword or the rope? Would I like a bloody death, swift and clean, or to be hanged, drawn and quartered? Tell me, Edward. Would you watch while they pull out my entrails? Would you keep my heart? Preserve it for old times' sake, eh?"

"George, please!" Edward's voice quavered.

"Too gruesome for you, brother? You have seen gore enough on the battlefield. But wait, it is your brother we are talking about. Your brother whom you have condemned to death. Let's see, how about drowning me in a vat of Malmsey wine? Just hold my head in that. Mmm, an expensive sweet wine. Sounds good to me."

"Be serious, George…"

"Oh, but I am. I am very serious. I'd rather have a few gulps of your precious wine as I go on my way to the Almighty. Sounds so much better than being hanged, your inners torn out or having one's head cut off. Don't you think? Indeed, I am deadly serious. He laughed again at his pun.

Edward instructed his guards to get on with the job. He wanted no more of it. George had refused to be serious. He was no wiser whether George knew about his bigamy. The black cloud of depression fell, engulfing him. It grieved him to murder his brother, but he was too dangerous to be allowed to live.

George, Duke of Clarence, was put to death on 18th February 1478. He was buried in Tewkesbury Abbey alongside his wife, Isabel. Richard, Duke of Gloucester, stood in the shadow to hide the tears that refused to be quelled. He had loved his brother and felt the guilt of his part in his death. George had been a traitor; it was true, but couldn't there have been another way?

Queen Elizabeth was delighted that, at last, George had paid the ultimate price for his part in the death of her father and brother. She felt safe at last. Her known enemies had all been removed. Even the Duchess of Norfolk was silenced. Her daughter now married to Edward's son; she would hardly want to discredit the family. It was a blessing the Duchess had removed herself to Norfolk and become almost a recluse.

Richard, Duke of Gloucester, had become rather bothersome. Since George's death, he had hardly spoken to her. He acted as if it were she who had committed treason. He was distantly polite, but she had caught him on several occasions glaring at her when he thought she could not observe him. There was a look in his eye that disturbed her. He had politely refused several invitations to dine with them, claiming he was needed in the north. Edward had given him sole responsibility for the north, almost like his own little kingdom. It infuriated her. Edward gave his young brother a ridiculous amount of power. When she questioned it, Edward became enraged. She shivered as she remembered the scene. "Do you dare to question your king, madam?" His face was white, and eyes were inflamed. "Are you attacking my younger brother now you have George out of the way? Isn't that enough for you?" He bared his teeth, resembling a wild animal. She was afraid. She had never seen Edward in such a rage. "I would trust Richard with my life! I trust him with the life of my sons! If it hadn't been for Richard..." He sank into a chair, clutching his head with both hands and let out a prolonged mournful cry, the cry of a wounded animal. Then he spoke almost in a whisper. "And Richard also feels the pain, the guilt of taking the life of our brother. All because of me."

Elizabeth had not known what to do. She had made a move towards him. But he thrust out his hand. "Begone! Leave me to suffer my guilt on my own. Oh, Eleanor, Eleanor. I am the most hateful man." She had heard the anguish of his tormented soul. Why had he called on Eleanor? She wasn't the one who had supported him all these years or had born his children. Elizabeth was amazed at how one could hate and love a man at the same time.

The death of George left its mark on Edward. He often became morose. When his moods became dark, people feared him. But it was not just his guilt about George that tormented him. Edward had dreams, dreams that left him weak. He dreamt of Eleanor and how he had loved her. He reached out to take her in his arms, but she faded away. She was always so elusive. He saw her young and beautiful. Once, she carried a babe in her arms. Was it his son? Eleanor never told him whether he lived or died. His dreams became more frequent. They tormented him and thrilled him at the same time. Every night when he went to bed, he wasn't sure whether he wanted Eleanor to visit him in his dreams or not.

Then one night, she appeared lying beside him. He reached out to touch her. She smiled. He withdrew his hand. He didn't deserve to touch her. He whispered. "Oh, my darling. Why did I treat you so badly? Was it our son you held in your arms?" She laughed. "That babe is my sister's. His little soul is with me. Our son is alive and well, Edward. I didn't tell you because I feared for his safety." He was disappointed to hear such words, but he understood. He had betrayed her trust before. Why would she ever trust him again? He opened his heart to her.

"How I wish I had acted differently, Eleanor. It is my greatest regret that I never met my son. I would not have hurt him, but I understand there are others who would." Eleanor put her hand on his face. Such a gentle touch, a soft breath of air on his cheek. He wondered if she felt the unmanly tears. She said nothing. "Tell me, Eleanor, does he live? Is it too late to do something for him? It is my wish to make him an earl, to give him an income. I want to provide for my son." He watched as her image faded. Then he saw she was standing at the bedside, but he knew she was leaving. He felt such sadness. In a gentle voice, she said, "If you wish to see your son Edward, visit my sister Elizabeth. He will be there, and he will tell you if he wishes to be an earl. Go to the house in Norfolk where you last saw me. That is where you will find her."

He awoke. It was another dream, but so real. He lay there wondering if Eleanor really visited him in his dreams. Then he decided. He would go to Norfolk. He would find out if Eleanor had really been with him. He left early in the morning and told no one but his steward that he was going but did not say where. His horse was ready. It would take time, but it was an easy ride.

Two days later, he reached his destination at East Hall,

Kenninghall, Norfolk. He recalled his last visit so long ago. Eleanor had greeted him coldly, but they had parted with a passionate kiss. Once again, the bell echoed through the house. He waited and rang again. Footsteps came closer, and a nun opened the door. He wasn't sure if she was the same person. She didn't seem surprised to see him, simply curtsied and stood back for him to enter. "The Duchess is waiting, your majesty. May I show you the way?" He blushed, remembering how rudely he had pushed her aside last time. He didn't need to reply; she was walking ahead. Perplexed, he wondered how it was that Elizabeth expected him. The nun turned and, seeing he hadn't moved, waited.

Elizabeth was in the same room where he had met Eleanor. She rose and gave a deep curtsy. 'Your majesty." But Edward was not looking at her. Standing next to her was a young man, his very image. He paled. There was no question who he was. Edward could find no words. The young gentleman bowed. Still, Edward did not speak. Elizabeth, amused at the king's silence, spoke. "Your majesty, may I present Edward Plantagenet de Wigmore. Edward, this is King Edward, your father." The young man bowed his head. "I am very pleased to meet you, your majesty." His voice was strong and confident. Still, Edward was speechless. Elizabeth, by now, asked if she could be seated. The king apologised and signalled for her to sit.

Edward had no idea how Elizabeth had known he was coming.

He didn't dare ask. He was fascinated. He could see himself in his son. He soon realised young Edward was well educated and had been brought up as a gentleman. He wanted to ask if his son expected to be his heir but refrained from asking such questions. He told him that he had prepared documents that made him the Earl of Ely from that day. There is a grand manor, a very good living and 200 acres of forest. Young Edward met his eyes. The king saw Eleanor's eyes looking into his own. He felt uneasy. His son spoke.

"For years, I believed I was a son of the church. It is only very recently that I have learned I am the son of a king, who deserted both my mother and me. I learned when I was very young that my mother had died, but there was no mention of a father. The only relative that I was aware of is my aunt here. She has been there for me all my life."

Edward began to feel uncomfortable. "You were kept from me." His son interrupted him. "Your majesty, father. I do not intend to be critical of either of my parents. It is God you will make your peace with. I simply want to tell you I am not interested in fighting for a throne. It belongs to you and your sons, my brothers. My existence quite possibly would be an embarrassment to you. In fact, I understand it could topple the queen and her children, who would become illegitimate. My mother would not have wished that. I am quite content to make my own way in life.

My wish, like you, is to serve others. I do not need to be a king to do that."

Edward sat back. How he admired this son of his. How proud he was. It made him feel so humble. He could see that although Eleanor was not alive, she lived within her son.

"Am I to understand that you do not wish me to acknowledge you as my son?"

"That is correct." Young Edward's reply was decisive. "It was my mother's wish that I meet you and understand my heritage. We can be happy in that knowledge."

The king sat thinking. His son was right. To acknowledge him would invalidate his marriage. His other sons would become bastards. But how happy he was to meet him at last. Eleanor had forgiven and trusted him to meet their son. He would not let her down again. He would ask nothing of young Edward. Just let him enjoy his life. He owed him that.

"Will you accept the Earldom? He hoped his son would allow him that privilege.

"I will. But only on the condition that you call me by the name I have answered to all my life. I am known as Giles Plantagenet, although registered as Edward Plantagenet de Wigmore.

The King was satisfied. He stood, and his son did the same. King Edward laughed. He could see himself. How could the likeness be explained? He was the king. He didn't have to explain anything. One thing he knew for certain, he would make sure that Elizabeth, his queen, did not find out he existed. He would keep Giles away from court.

King Edward told no one about his son. He was happy. His son became known as Lord Giles Plantagenet, Earl of Ely. Edward had met Giles at his new property and ensured he had the staff to manage it. His Aunt Elizabeth had also given him advice and stayed with him for some time until she was satisfied he was comfortable. Edward no longer dreamt of Eleanor; he felt at peace.

It was spring. Edward sat on the bank of the river, holding his rod and waiting for a catch. He enjoyed such rare times when he could leave his worries at his castle and enjoy nature with a few friends. It was a simple life. Surely the life of a peasant must be sweet at times. Sometimes he envied them and their way of life. How good it would be not to have the concerns of the country. He watched the daffodils gently swaying in the breeze, their bright yellow competing with the sun. It had been an enjoyable fishing trip on the Thames. But he was tired, so tired. In a few days, he would return to his palace; his peace would be over,

Spring is a fickle season, and in a day, the weather suddenly changed. So much rain and wind with a chill that froze him to the bone, and howled like an animal in pain. The fishing trip came to a sudden end.

Back at his palace, Edward couldn't get warm. He cursed the cold and held his head that throbbed. He had caught a cold. His doctors insisted he went to bed. He was thankful. Bed had never been so welcome. How strange he should be so tired after the fishing trip.

That night he dreamed of Eleanor again. She stood framed in the window, an ethereal figure standing in a pool of light from the moon. She smiled, stretched out her arms and walked towards him. "Come, Edward, it is time." He didn't hesitate but gladly walked into her arms.

Edward's sudden death shocked the court. Elizabeth rushed to his room. He looked so peaceful. She felt angry. Why had he left her so soon? He was not yet 41. Their son was so young. She would need to hurry and take charge before others did. She turned and walked out of the room. King Edward V must be crowned as soon as possible.

Queen Elizabeth was at her wit's end. No one had expected the death of the King. Her son, the Prince of Wales, was at Ludlow with his uncle Anthony Woodville. Elizabeth had not expected young Edward, only twelve years old, to become king. Her anger turned to blame. She blamed Edward for dying so suddenly and before his son was of age. Their son was too young to rule effectively but too old for a minority. It was most inconvenient for Edward to die at this time.

Elizabeth knew her husband would expect his brother Richard Duke of Gloucester, to be Lord Protector. He admired his brother, who had an outstanding record of service to the crown. She had not the slightest doubt it would be his wish. But it certainly did not suit her, and she was determined that power would not pass to Richard. She would have to work quickly to get her son to Windsor. Richard was in the north. She would make sure he did not receive the news of the death of his brother in a hurry.

Chapter 12

Richard, Duke of Gloucester, stared at the messenger whose horse was wet from its hard ride. He watched as the man staggered from his horse and stumbled toward him, bowing and holding his sealed parchment. He could see that the messenger was near collapse, and he signalled to one of his men to attend to him. He recognised the seal from William Lord Hastings, chamberlain and close friend of his brother King Edward. As his eyes roamed over the content, his face turned pale.

"*The king, your brother is dead. He died unexpectedly on 9th April. The Woodville's are keeping this news from you while they seize power. They are determined you will not be protector or the young king's guardian. Young King Edward V is at Ludlow with*

Elizabeth knew her husband would expect his brother Richard Duke of Gloucester, to be Lord Protector. He admired his brother, who had an outstanding record of service to the crown. She had not the slightest doubt it would be his wish. But it certainly did not suit her, and she was determined that power would not pass to Richard. She would have to work quickly to get her son to Windsor. Richard was in the north. She would make sure he did not receive the news of the death of his brother in a hurry.

Chapter 12

Richard, Duke of Gloucester, stared at the messenger whose horse was wet from its hard ride. He watched as the man staggered from his horse and stumbled toward him, bowing and holding his sealed parchment. He could see that the messenger was near collapse, and he signalled to one of his men to attend to him. He recognised the seal from William Lord Hastings, chamberlain and close friend of his brother King Edward. As his eyes roamed over the content, his face turned pale.

"The king, your brother is dead. He died unexpectedly on 9th April. The Woodville's are keeping this news from you while they seize power. They are determined you will not be protector or the young king's guardian. Young King Edward V is at Ludlow with

his uncle Anthony Woodville. They intend to return to London in haste to thwart you."

At first, he felt nothing but deep sorrow. Edward gone, snuffed like a flame in the wind. No goodbye. Richard felt his knees weaken. A numbness crept over him. He stumbled. One of his men stopped his fall and led the duke inside his manor. Whatever news Richard had received was bad. Once inside his manor, Richard read the message again. His mood of sorrow turned to anger. What could the Queen be thinking keeping the news of Edward's death from him?

She was aware that Edward would want him to take charge of his nephew, but once again, the greedy Woodvilles were out to grab power. He needed to be as cunning as they. No matter what it took, he would relieve Woodville of the young king and arrange his coronation. What is more, he understood the Queen was his enemy. It was important that he, the late king's brother, should show his loyalty to young King Edward and present himself as the defender of his brother to protect the late king's achievements of stability against the plotting of the Woodvilles.

Richard sent his spies south in haste. It was reported that a Privy Council assembled in London immediately after Edward's death. The queen dowager insisted the young king should be escorted by a strong body of followers. Hasting was opposed to the idea but finally agreed to an escort of 2000. Sunday, 4th May, was appointed for the coronation. Richard learned the Queen and her friends distrusted both him and Buckingham. He was not surprised. He no more trusted the queen than she trusted him. Richard also suspected that the haste to get young Edward to London was a ruse by Rivers and his party to keep Edward in the hands of the Woodvilles.

The Duke of Buckingham arranged to meet Richard, Duke of Gloucester, at Northampton. The young king had already passed through Northampton when Richard arrived and was ten miles further on the road to London, stopping at Stony Stratford. Lord Rivers and Lord Grey, who had accompanied young Edward, had ridden back to welcome Richard on behalf of the king. The Duke of Buckingham, who had just arrived, strode towards them, suggesting they sup together. Despite the cordial conversation, there was an undercurrent of distrust between each party. Richard was pleased when Rivers and Grey departed and immediately invited Sir Richard Ratcliffe and Lord Stanley to join him and Buckingham for consultation on what their next move would be.

Buckingham informed Richard of the latest news from London. Then leaned forward confidentially and spoke in a hushed voice. "The goings-on and secret meetings seem downright suspicious to me." Ratcliffe nodded his head. "Everything is done with haste. Even the coronation has been fixed surprisingly early, on 4th May, isn't it? The King will be lucky to have reached London by then."

Richard looked grim. Stanley spoke.

"They wanted a formidable body of retainers, but Hastings was absolutely against the idea."

Richard chortled. "They would have reached London far more quickly without the 2000 followers that are undoubtedly an encumbrance to them." There were a few sniggers. Then Buckingham raised his voice. "The truth of the matter is Elizabeth, the Queen Dowager, doesn't want you, Richard, to get power over her son. She says his father would not have wished it." Richard smiled. "Elizabeth knows full well Edward, my brother, had spoken of the matter on more than one occasion. It was the will of the king that after his death, the care of his son's person and kingdom be transferred to me, Richard, Duke of Gloucester. He was particularly worried when Clarence was alive that he could not be trusted to protect Edward. Still, all that is behind us. It will not be long before the king will be of age. In the meantime, tomorrow, I will ensure I speak to my nephew myself and then escort him to resume his journey to London to meet his people.

Buckingham yawned and rose from his chair. "It's bed for me. I suggest we rise at first dawn, Richard, if we are to catch the worm." Richard stood and stretched. It had been a long day, and he had no doubt the morrow would be equally challenging. He had given the word to his followers that an early start was necessary. He was pleased he had taken the precaution of securing the keys to the inn. Both he and Buckingham felt the need to be one step ahead of Rivers and Grey. They were suspicious the young king would be rushed to London to the hands of the queen's party.

The Earl was infuriated by the extraordinary measures the dukes had taken to prevent him from continuing his journey with the king and demanded answers. Richard answered curtly. He accused Rivers of deliberately keeping distance between himself and his nephew, the king and arrested him on the spot. The dukes rushed to Stony Stratford just in time to obtain an audience with the young king before he continued his journey.

Richard bowed to his nephew. "My liege, it is with great sorrow I have the need to tell you of the deceit and wickedness of your uncle Lord Rivers and your half-brothers. Edward looked alarmed and confused. Richard continued. "They have plotted to seize the government and take the power of the old nobility." Edward stared, fingering his sleeve."

"I am sure you are wrong, misinformed…" his voice began to tremble. "I can vouch for my Uncle Rivers and brother. They are innocent of such acts." The Duke of Buckingham spoke kindly. "Ah, my liege, it is terrible, terrible that they have deceived you so and kept these matters from your ears."

Edward lowered his head and said nothing. He did not want his Uncle Gloucester to see his tears. He didn't know what to think or do. It was too much. Why did his father have to leave him so soon?

He wasn't ready to be king. He gulped, trying to keep calm and not show them how terribly frightened he was. Richard looked at the sorrowful figure of his nephew. He, too, wasn't sure what to do. He wanted to put a hand on the boy's shoulder and reassure him, but it wouldn't do to touch him. He must show deference to his nephew, who was, after all, his king. He remembered how difficult it was as a boy of twelve or thirteen to be thrust into a man's world. Everyone expected so much from you. He looked down at his young nephew again and spoke with gentleness. "Aye, my liege, it is time to retire. We have a long journey tomorrow. Your people are anxious to swear fealty to you."

It was Lord Hastings who calmed the storm when the news reached London of the king taken on his journey and his Uncle Rivers and brother's arrest. Richard had made sure he had been informed of what had happened. The lords met, and Hastings advised them what had happened. The king was safe. Rivers had been believed to be involved in a conspiracy against Gloucester and Buckingham. Arrests had been made to protect the dukes. Both Gloucester and Buckingham were on their way to London for the coronation. It would all be sorted soon.

Elizabeth was not convinced. When she heard of the arrests, she was fearful. Once again, she sought sanctuary at Westminster. Fear fed her anger, and she admonished her servants for taking so long to bring her property to her at the abbey. No matter the

Archbishop of York tried to assure her that Hastings had explained everything. All would be well. Nothing would be done that she was opposed to. The king was safe, and no harm threatened him. Everything would end well. Elizabeth restrained herself from calling him a fool. He then placed the Great Seal of England in her hands but almost immediately realised that he had committed a great violation of the trust imposed on him and hastily asked for it back. Elizabeth said nothing, but with a withering look, she handed it to him.

When Elizabeth heard that the Dukes Gloucester and Buckingham had ordered the seizure of Rivers and his party's baggage and had discovered large quantities of barrels containing armour and implements of war, she despaired. Rivers and his party were seen to be found guilty. The shocking news spread. 'It were alms to hang the traitors.' She knew Gloucester and Buckingham would show no mercy.

The young king arrived at Hornsea Park with his uncle Gloucester and the Duke of Buckingham.

Chapter 13

"I don't have time for the power-hungry Woodvilles. They are so anxious to keep the young king from the hands of Richard that they organised Edward's funeral before the duke can get to London." Collingbourne was with Walter Hungerford, in the great chamber in his manor at Lydiad. Hungerford accepted the mug of ale Collingbourne offered him. His thin face looked serious. "I understand Edward's nephew, John, Earl of Lincoln, has taken the Duke of Gloucester's place as chief mourner." Collingbourne seated himself in one of the tapestried chairs. The sun suddenly burst through the tall windows, highlighting raindrops trickling to the bottom of the glass. He was fascinated by the way one drop joined another, gathering speed in the race to the bottom. April was a fickle month. Sunshine followed by rain. He turned his attention to his guest. "I wonder what Edward would have made of it that his only brother was deliberately prevented from attending his funeral? The funeral could wait until Richard reaches London, but clearly, that doesn't suit the queen. I heard that she deliberately did not inform Richard of the king's death. It was Hastings who eventually informed him advising him that the Woodville's were doing all they could to seize power." Collingbourne didn't add that it was Margaret, Countess of Richmond, who had given him that interesting piece of news. The countess was in a good position to know what was going on with her husband, Lord Thomas Stanley, at court.

"You've got to be careful, William," Walter spoke slowly. "Can you trust the Countess? She seems to have one aim in life: to get her son on the throne." Collingbourne gave a forced laugh. "Oh, she's no fool. She just likes to know what is going on. She wouldn't do anything foolish and certainly would not involve me." Walter shook his head. "I know you are besotted with her, my friend, but what you say is true, she is no fool, and that is what concerns me." Collingbourne guffawed. Walter drained his mug of ale and changed the subject.

"I've written to young King Edward requesting an annuity – My oath William I have been a faithful servant to his father." Collingbourne shuffled his feet. "I know. We all do our best."

"Hmm...but it's paid off for you." Walter began to scowl. "Look at you! Own nearly half of Wiltshire and Somerset, and you've property in London. You've got Ludgershall as well. Edward was good to you."

William fumed, his face going red. "Hold on there, Walter, old boy. It's not all from the crown, you know. I inherited some of it. A good dowry came with Margaret, my wife. The rest I have worked hard for. The administrative work I have done has not been easy, as you well know. I have spent hours working for the late king – why the Duke of Clarence's death alone meant months of research with the Duke of Gloucester."

"Yes...yes..but it had its compensations. The truth was you had the king's ear, and that gave you power, William. You cannot deny that. How much property has been passed your way by a certain bishop in return for your lobbying?" Walter tapped his fingers on the arm of his chair. Then he continued. "You were favoured by Edward. But my family has nothing to thank him for." He scowled. He was thinking that Edward had not been on the throne for long when he had granted all the Hungerford estates he held to his brother Richard Duke of Gloucester. Then in 1468, Sir Thomas Hungerford was seized, and imprisoned at Salisbury. He and his friends tried before Richard of Gloucester, who was only sixteen then, condemned then hanged, drawn and quartered. With the thoughts in his mind, his voice bitter, he muttered, "I still don't believe Thomas was guilty of conspiring against the King."

Collingbourne said nothing. He knew what Walter was referring to. The two men sat silent for a while. Walter spoke his thoughts. "We had two attainders within eight years and the loss of many titles and lands! But that wasn't enough. He had to have Farleigh as well."

"That was your family seat, wasn't it?" Collingbourne gave a stifled yawn.

"And he got Heytesbury and Teffont!" Walter's face was turning red. "I know you are a Yorkist through and through, but I have nothing to thank Edward for or Richard. "I just hope young King Edward treats us better." Walter changed his tone. Have you received your black gown for Edward's funeral? I heard you were one of the ushers at Windsor. I was charged to help move the coffin into the King's private chapel in Westminster Palace."

Collingbourne nodded. He had already been to pay his respects to his dear friend and king. The coffin was draped in black, and hundreds of candles flickered throughout the chapel. A Requiem was sung by Edward Story, the Bishop of Chichester. William was struck by a deep sadness as the Bishop's voice soared. Life was like a candle in the wind – a fragile and vulnerable thing. His turn to kneel outside the hearse of his friend was to be at Windsor Castle on 18th April. There he would join forty to fifty others, including lords and knights, to take part in a watch throughout the night. On the following morning, the ceremonies would be completed but William had been told that the men who had stood within or knelt without the hearse during the night watch would depart for some rest.

Chapter 14

Margaret, Countess of Richmond, sat running a finger around the rim of her goblet of wine on a beautiful day in June. She was sitting in the rose garden at Lydiad, thinking about the scandalous happenings that brought about the shocking execution of Sir William Hastings and the injury that her husband, Lord Thomas Stanley, had received. The Duke of Gloucester had claimed he had unveiled a plot whereby Hastings was acting in concert with the Queen Dowager and organised a confederacy to destroy himself and the Duke of Buckingham. She had learned what had happened from her husband Thomas, who had a blow aimed at his head with a pole-axe. Fortunately, he had ducked and received a slight injury to his face. He was taken into custody.

When she heard the news, she immediately insisted on seeing her husband. She paid a high bribe to do so. He looked pale, clearly suffering from shock, and a jagged cut showed dried blood on his face. Angrily, she called for water and linen to clean it. He said he had no idea what had gotten into Richard. As she dabbed at the cut, he spoke, wincing in between words as she had patted at the wound. "Earlier, he (the Duke) had been of good humour. He had left the chamber for a while then came back scowling with a look like thunder." He winced again. "Armed men rushed into the room, calling out treason. There was confusion. None of us knew what was going on. The others, Bishop of Ely and Archbishop of York, were also marched out of the chamber. I have no idea what happened after that until much later. Richard himself came to speak to me. He said how shocked he was to hear of the betrayal of Hastings, and he would deal with me when he found out more."

The Countess frowned and took a sip of her wine. It was sweet and delicious. She leaned back on her chair, enjoying the warm sunshine. She closed her eyes. A kiss on the cheek startled her. Collingbourne was smiling, shaking his head. He playfully wagged a finger at her. "Is this what you get up to while I am away on business for you?" He sat beside her, thanked the servant who had already brought refreshment, and placed it on the ornate table.

"Did you succeed?" she leaned forward, eager to receive his news.

"Oh yes. I spoke to Richard himself. He assures me your dear husband is safe for the moment, at least. He claims that men such as Hastings, Rotherham, Moreton and your husband Stanley were the heart of Edward's government. They clearly disliked being moved to the periphery. The Duke contends this same little group also resented the Duke of Buckingham gaining power they once believed was theirs. Seems like one of Hasting's followers had a word in Richard's ear, and as a result, Buckingham consorted with a few of them to sound their intentions. Richard wouldn't say what, but he did assure me that they discovered an incipient conspiracy.

"But how could Richard execute Hastings, who had been a close friend of his brother? And wasn't it he who informed Richard that his brother, the king was dead when the queen failed to do so? How loyal is that?"

"It must have been a difficult call for him." Collingbourne looked thoughtful. "Both Hastings and Richard were there for Edward when he fled for his life to Burgundy and again at Barnett. They were both loyal to Edward. He probably would not have got his crown back without them. He shook his head, confused, then turned toward the table and licked his lips

"That was very tasty. I didn't realise I was so hungry." He looked longingly at the remaining food, then patted his stomach. "I'd better not." Margaret laughed but agreed with him.

"The problem for Richard was he had to choose between Hastings and Buckingham. I believe Richard was well aware Buckingham was a fly in the ointment. He had heard mumblings that Buckingham advertised the fact he was the Protector's friend, his ally. Buckingham had much to say in the council chamber, in fact; some complained they had got rid of the Woodville party to be replaced by another – the Party of the Protectorate. As much as Richard loved Hastings and remembered the close friendship he had shared with the late king, he could not afford to sacrifice Buckingham."

Margaret sighed. "Did you ask why he has imprisoned Thomas?" Collingbourne took her hand. "My love, I have to admit I rather enjoy Thomas in prison. It gives me time with you." She pulled her hand away. "Be serious, William. We cannot afford to offend Richard; he has the young King's ear." William laughed. "You are deliciously immoral and quite calculating." She pouted but was anxious for his answer. "If you want the truth, I believe you are the problem." She looked startled. Collingbourne laughed. "You find that difficult to believe? My dearest, apart from the fact that Stanley has a capacity for disloyalty if it suits him, he is married to you – a Lancastrian Pretender's mother." Margaret frowned and spoke sharply. "That is unkind, William."

He tried to take her hand, but she moved aside. "Margaret, everyone knows you will do anything to see your son Henry on the throne of England. Didn't you tell me yourself your marriage to Stanley is a marriage of convenience? Convenient for you to be invited to court and get closer to your dream. You know in the end that Stanley will do what best benefits him; you are just hoping you can persuade him that supporting your son is just that." Margaret twisted her lips, she knew it was the truth, but she didn't like the fact that William could see it so clearly. She was determined that he, too, would change his allegiance and help her get Henry on the throne.

Within days Thomas Stanley was released and restored to his place in the council. It seemed Richard trusted him, but the truth was Richard was well aware that to do otherwise could result in repercussions from Lord Strange, Stanley's son, who was a threat in Lancashire. Margaret was delighted. She was well informed that her husband was involved in the conspiracy against Richard, although he had not confided in her. She was amused that he admitted that there was a case for Richard's concern with Hastings. As much as she tried to question him, he was reluctant to talk. He wanted to keep her out of it. He had given his word to Richard that she had not been involved. That seemed enough for Richard. When she persisted in asking questions, he reluctantly spoke. "I didn't really have much to do with it all, but I knew something was afoot. Hastings was persuaded by his new mistress, Jane Shore, that if he intended to rule with the young king, he needed to change his attitude toward the queen dowager. They could plot together to eliminate the Protector and take power. She would be the go-between. No one would suspect her." He burst into loud laughter. "My oath, I am darned if I understand women. Seems she's a trusted spy and reports daily to the queen. Who would have thought that a likely relationship? The queen knew she was Edward's mistress. Edward said she hated her. Yet there they are scheming and plotting together like old friends."

"And what about John Morton, the Bishop of Ely?" Thomas stared at her for a moment; what was her interest in him?

"Buckingham has taken care of him in his castle at Brecknock."

"Do you know exactly what they were plotting?" Margaret knew she was pushing her luck. Stanley glowered.

"For God's sake, my Lady, let it be. No more questions. The least you know, the better. This is not a game. Richard is already wary of you, and probably with good reason. Do you think I am a fool? I know you spend every day of your life scheming to get your precious boy on the throne. It's not going to happen. We have a young king and a young Duke of York, heir to the throne, and if they don't manage to get there, Richard will." He strode out of the room to cool his anger. Margaret shrugged her shoulders. Anything was possible. Who would have thought the late king would have died at forty? Why, his boys might not even make adulthood, and the Duke of Gloucester? Well, admittedly, he was another matter, but no one was invincible. It was pleasing to her that Thomas was not as loyal to Richard as he would have her believe. Gradually, he was moving toward the Lancastrian movement. If her plans succeeded, it would not take much to push him over the edge and support Henry. But what of Buckingham? He had requested and been given custody of John Morton, the Bishop of Ely. She asked herself why Buckingham would wish to be his jailer at Brecknock. There was no one more zealous at plotting than Moreton, even in custody. She knew it would not be long before the bishop contacted her. He was as anxious as she for a Lancastrian restoration.

It was another beautiful day in June. A walk throughout the gardens was appealing. She walked towards the forests. Various shades of green contrasted with the blue sky. Late spring was a magnificent time of the year. Gone were the bare branches of winter, clusters of twigs, gnarled and twisted, extended like the very hands of old man winter now replaced by tiny leaves that uncurled, gradually dressing the trees in shades of green. It was good to be alive. Her thoughts turned to her husband's words. Jane Shore, a spy in the palace and now a spy for the queen dowager who was still in sanctuary. Elizabeth must be fearful and lonely, her world collapsing around her. Clearly, she distrusted Richard. Who could she turn to? Perhaps it was time she visited her friend.

Margaret could not understand that Elizabeth, the Queen Dowager, refused to leave sanctuary at Westminster Abbey. She was delighted that her visit had been welcomed by her. As she walked into the room, she was pleased to see that Elizabeth was living in comfort. She had heard it rumoured that the bishop had given up his own rooms for her use. Elizabeth was seated in a large tapestried chair. It was no surprise that she looked pale, her cheeks slightly sunken. Elizabeth acknowledged the curtsey Margaret had given and offered her a nearby chair.

"It is so pleasing to see you, Margaret." Elizabeth desired no formality. She had never really been sure whether Margaret was friend or foe. Edward had always warned her to be on her guard. Margaret was a doting mother who was very ambitious to see her son Henry at court. Through her husband, Thomas Stanley, she had made many appeals for Edward to pardon him. Edward had been reluctant. He didn't trust either Margaret or Henry. Elizabeth was aware that after Edward's death, a document was waiting for the king's signature that gave Henry the pardon Margaret had so desperately desired. It was unfortunate the king died before the matter was settled. She wondered if Margaret was aware of the fact and whether she would harass the young king to sign; it was not the time to ask Margaret about it now. She wondered what the purpose of her visit was. She waited for Margaret to speak.

Margaret smiled, trying not to show the pity she felt for

Elizabeth. She thought how devastating it must be that Elizabeth was separated from her son. This should be a time when she was by his side, giving him encouragement. She knew how difficult it was to be apart from your child. How often she had cried herself to sleep thinking of her son Henry, separated from her by necessity. She was fortunate that Jasper cared for him so well. But who did the young King Edward have? His Woodville relatives had been torn from his side. Even his brother kept from him. He was still so young. She looked directly at Elizabeth and spoke.

"Do you hear how the King fares?" Clearly, the question struck a chord. A look of pain spread over Elizabeth's face. Her voice quavered as she spoke.

"I understand he has not been well. He suffers from pain in his jaw." Her lips trembled. "The hardest thing is not being there to comfort him. Of course, he is grown now and would never admit he needs his mother, but you have a son, you understand; they are always your babes, especially when in pain. I fear for him. He has been too long without his family." Margaret put a hand on hers. "Is he being treated for the pain? I can send my own doctor to check on him if you wish. He is excellent." Elizabeth's eyes filled with tears.

"Would they let you?" Margaret waved her hand. "Pah! Of course. Richard will not refuse me such a request. I don't think he would be so cruel as to let Edward's son suffer." Elizabeth was not convinced, but there was hope.

"They want me to let my son Richard join him. I am fearful of allowing it, but those who defy Richard do not live long." She spoke with gritted teeth. "I have lost so many of my family and friends; perhaps it would be for the best to cooperate with him." Margaret tightened her lips. She reflected on her own position. It served no purpose to antagonise her enemies. She mumbled, "It is always wise to keep your enemies close." She lifted her voice, speaking more positively.

"It could be better for your boys to have each other's company at this difficult time. Soon Edward will be crowned and of age to rule in his own right. I understand he is an intelligent young man who has been well-educated. There will be no need for the Protectorate. Will you feel safe coming out of the sanctuary when that happens?

Elizabeth smiled. "I pray for that time and hope he will be a good king and son, but I have terrible dreams, Margaret. I do not see my son on the throne." She stood and began pacing the room. "How I miss my mother." Margaret remembered Jacquetta, the Duchess of Bedford's death not long after Edward had defeated the Lancastrians. It was said she died peacefully in her sleep at her home at Grafton. There were some who had rejoiced her passing. The witch was gone. There would be no more use of magic. Her thoughts were interrupted by Elizabeth's words. "I dreamt of my mother, Jacquetta. She told me I had much pain to bear. I will believe that God and his angels have forsaken me for all the sins I have committed in the past. I have been too vain, too proud and too cruel." She fought to keep control of her emotions. 'I have born so much pain already, but my mother says the worst is to come. I can't bear it!" Margaret felt her pain but said nothing allowing Elizabeth time to calm herself. Then she spoke. "Our Lord never gives us more than we can cope with. You must trust Him, Elizabeth. You will find your way through this storm, and the sun will shine on you once more. I will pray for you. You must be strong for your beautiful children."

Margaret kept her word. She approached Richard and told him of her visit to the Queen Dowager. Observing his surprise, she hurriedly added that she could not understand why Elizabeth should lock herself in the sanctuary. She chose her words carefully.

"Perhaps it is her grief that has made her think and act so foolishly." Richard stared as if trying to read her mind. "Ah, my Lady, how do you believe she acts so foolishly? Margaret understood he was testing her. He was seeking to find out what she knew. She simply smiled and spoke calmly. "Why, my Lord, what reason could there be for her to remain in the sanctuary with her children? Who would dream of harming them? Besides, the young king needs the company of his brother at this time. The sudden death of their father must be very difficult for them. The princesses also will not benefit from being locked in the abbey. It is no life for young girls. Why the eldest are young women who need fun and laughter, not locked up fearing for their lives."

Richard thought for a moment. He bit his lip. She was right. It was important he was not seen as a monster uncle to be feared. Already, his nephew, the young king, treated him coldly. He showed no affection and clearly blamed him for his mother fleeing to the sanctuary. He needed to repair his relationship with young Edward. It was his wish that he could guide him during his months of minority and continue to be there when he became of age. The boy must understand how loyal he had been to his father. How he respected him and how Edward had trusted him. He had hoped the same relationship could be developed between himself and young Edward. He frowned. He could see no likeness other than appearance in the boy with his father. He was a Woodville. Maybe one day, when he was older, he would understand that what had happened was a result of their greed and plotting. He, Richard, was doing his best to carry out Edward's wishes and protect the peace and stability of the country that Edward had worked so hard to achieve.

Margaret was watching the changing expressions on Richard's face. She could see he was struggling with his own thoughts. He was oblivious to her presence. Almost as if her thoughts reached him, he suddenly spoke.

"Yes, you may send your doctor to visit the king. So thoughtful. I would hope that those caring for him would have already sent for one. He needs to be well for his coronation. I agree with you. The Duke of York should be with him. As for the Queen Dowager, I have no idea why she remains in the abbey; quite irrational behavior, but I will continue to do my best to persuade her to at least release her daughters." He turned to go, then looked back. "Thank you, my lady, for your concern, but do not think I am fooled by you. Stanley assures me you are innocent of any plotting. I know otherwise. Take care you do not go too far.

Chapter 15

Richard had thought long and hard before he had destroyed Hastings. He had never sought power or greatness. It had been thrust on him by his brother, Edward. Richard had done his best to serve Edward loyally all his life. He, therefore, considered Hasting's conspiracy as the highest insult ever. He was undermining his loyalty to his brother, the late king, by suggesting that he could not be trusted to see young Edward crowned king. Well aware that Hasting's intention was to get rid of him as Protector, he realised that Hastings and his party planned to govern in young Edward's name. This knowledge had come to his ears when he was still contemplating on another piece of news that had astounded him.

He had been surprised when Robert Stillingham, Bishop of Bath and Wells, sought a hearing to his ears alone. He had important intelligence that it was crucial he heard. When the Bishop arrived, Richard received him alone. Sitting opposite, Richard noted how nervous the Bishop appeared. He fiddled with his ring, wrung his hands, and remained speechless until Richard encouraged him to speak. The Bishop began, stopped, then started again. Finally, he came straight to the point. "The King and the young Duke of York have no rightful claim to the throne." He gave a huge sigh and leaned back in his chair. Richard, quite stunned, waited for more. The Bishop began fidgeting in his chair and then spoke again. "My lord, Elizabeth was not Edward's lawful wife. I had been sworn never to speak of it while the late King Edward was alive, but now, since his death, I can no longer conceal the truth and expect God's mercy."

Richard remembered that once Clarence had whispered something similar, but he had thought it was spite because Edward had charged him with high treason.

"How have you come by this preposterous conclusion?" Richard's voice was cold but calm.

"I performed the service myself." Richard's face drained white. "You did, and you have kept silent all these years. Why?"

"I daren't speak, my Lord, not while his liege King Edward lived. He said I had a choice. To be well rewarded, or hanged drawn and quartered for treason."

"Do you have any proof of this? Were there any witnesses?" Richard had arisen from his chair and was looking out of the window.

He turned when Stillington had not answered, waiting.

"My Lord, there were those who knew, but no other witness of the ceremony. The king would not have it so."

Richard drew a breath and said under his breath. "I bet he wouldn't."

"I believed the King loved her. It wasn't a hasty promise said in the moment. He planned the date and asked me to be there."

"Who was she? Richard knew that Edward loved the ladies. He wondered which of his fancy pieces this woman was.

"She was a lady, my Lord. Lady Eleanor Talbot, daughter of Earl Talbot." Richard stood, quite shocked. Memories stirred from deep within. Wasn't that the sister of Elizabeth, Duchess of Norfolk? Her young daughter, Anne Mowbray, had been married to the young Duke of York. He had inherited all her lands when she died a few years later. He wanted to hear no more from this man.

"Thank you for this information. We will speak no more until I have considered the situation."

Stillingham stood, bowed and left the room, relieved the ordeal was over. The Duke could do with it what he wished. His soul was saved.

Richard did nothing with the knowledge for a few days. Finally, he disclosed it to his inner council. Buckingham was delighted with the news. He urged Richard to use it. He had already suggested the realm needed a man. Not a wimp of a boy who was tied to his Woodville relatives. Richard was popular and had proved that he could rule wisely and fairly in his management of the north. He was the best man for the position. He, for one, was willing to serve him. Lord Howard was also vocal in supporting Buckingham's support. Richard was no fool. They all had their own vested interest in supporting Buckingham. Howard, for instance, had missed out on claiming the dukedom of Norfolk through his mother because the late King had arranged the marriage of the child heiress Lady Anne Mowbray to his son, the young Duke of York. Lady Anne Mowbray was dead now, so it was very much in Howard's interest to champion Buckingham's pleas.

Richard's greatest surprise was William Catesby, who quietly said he had a need to speak to him in private. Richard suggested he call at his home later that afternoon. When they sat alone, Catesby unburdened his story. He said that, as Richard would know, Eleanor was a relative of his through marriage. He had received a letter from her asking him to visit her urgently as she required some legal documentation prepared. When he arrived, she was very distressed, so unlike her. She wished to tell him a secret that she said could cost him his life if he ever told another soul. "You can imagine how dumbfounded I was when she told me she was married to Edward shortly after he became king. The marriage ceremony carried out and witnessed by a priest." Catesby paused, shaking his head as even now he realised how absurd it sounded. "I wondered whether the lady had lost her mind and warned that such words were dangerous. She insisted it was true."

Richard searched Catesby's face. This was a man whom he absolutely trusted, but he needed clarification. "Why was the marriage kept secret?"

"I asked her the same thing, and she said Edward claimed he wanted to wait until he had found the right moment to tell Warwick." He shook his head. "If you remember, Warwick was negotiating for a French bride. Maybe he married Eleanor so he couldn't be forced into marrying a woman of Warwick's choice." Richard grunted. He knew his brother could be infuriatingly obstinate if pushed into a corner. Warwick believed he had placed Edward on the throne, thus he should be eternally grateful and guided by him, but Edward was very much his own man. He had no intention of allowing Warwick to dictate the terms of his reign.

"Then why in heavens name didn't he admit he was married then and tell Warwick to get on with it?" Richard began to pace the room, scowling. It made no sense to him at all.

"I have no idea; Eleanor was a lady any man would be proud to have as his wife, beautiful, intelligent and well-bred. He didn't even tell her he had married Elizabeth. He kept it secret for a few months. I daresay he had to do it in private in case Eleanor challenged the marriage. She was, after all, an Earl's daughter and daughter-in-law to Lord Sudeley. There was plenty of support from very influential people." He accepted the mug of ale Richard offered.

They both sat for a few minutes mulling over what had been said. Then Catesby spoke again.

"Eleanor said she was shocked and profoundly hurt when his marriage to Elizabeth Woodville was announced. Although she had made no attempt to challenge the marriage, she knew her life was in danger. That is why she asked me to prepare a deed of gift in favour of her sister Elizabeth, Duchess of Norfolk, in June 1468. She wanted Fenny Compton conveyed to Elizabeth with absolute immediate effect. King Edward had recently visited her to warn her that it would be to her peril if she challenged his marriage to Elizabeth, his queen. She and her mother, Jacquetta, had been informed of the truth and were determined to extinguish it. Seems she was right; within weeks, she was dead."

It saddened Richard to learn such news. Whatever had made Edward do such a thing? It was one thing to take a mistress. He had himself, but not since he married Anne. Why did Edward marry her in secret? She, a respectable noblewoman of good birth? Why did he betray her? He was not sure he wanted to know. And Edward's boys, one already declared king and waiting to be crowned, what was he to do about them? They were innocent. They did not deserve what was to happen to them, but how could he stand back and allow the coronation when he knew it was wrong? For the first time in his life, he cursed his brother and his wanton ways. As for Elizabeth, despite his anger, he understood that if she believed Edward was a bachelor and free to marry her, how devastating it must have been to discover the truth. What a terrible position Edward had put her. What could she do? She feared she would be cast aside and her children would become bastards. She must have been terrified. But if she had been guilty of murdering Edward's wife, what guilt she carried now? He had no desire to discuss the situation with her. What could she say? Admit her guilt or lie?

He did, however, instruct that the Queen Dowager release the young Duke of Norfolk from the sanctuary. His instructions were to allow her to hand him over willingly, but if she refused, take him by force. He has no right to the sanctuary, and his brother needs him.

Elizabeth had been expecting the visit and demand for her son. She sensed it was a fait accompli; there was no use fighting it any more. She reluctantly handed her young son to the Cardinal Archbishop, the Lord Chancellor and a deputation of other lords. They were met by the Duke of Buckingham in Westminster Hall. Richard watched as his little nephew, looking bewildered, walked towards him. A mixture of different emotions struggled from deep within him to the surface. Sadness, joy, fear, sorrow, pity and guilt. He bent and embraced him affectionately, taking longer than intended to try to stop the tears that were determined to fall from his eyes.

They proceeded to the Tower, and Gloucester observed the joy on the young king's face as he spotted his brother. Young Edward glanced up at his Uncle Richard Gloucester and smiled. It was the first smile Richard had received from him. He vowed, whatever happened, his nephews would not suffer. They would not be parted again. They were innocent, and he did not intend to offer them as a sacrifice. Didn't his position as Protector include them? He cursed his brother Edward again. What a position he had put him.

That night Richard dreamed. He tossed and turned in his bed. He yelled out, such a howling of despair that Anne, his wife, sat up concerned. His nightgown was soaked by perspiration. She called to his man for cool water and linen. Together they removed the soaking robe, and she lovingly cooled his body with the scented water. She didn't speak, she just allowed him to relieve the tension with tears and sobs. Finally, when he was calmed and had been given a herbal sedative, he spoke. "Edward's boys are in danger. I saw their bodies mutilated; their blood spilt on the coverlets." He grabbed her arm. "Say it isn't true. It mustn't be true." He began to weep.

Anne lay beside him, holding him in her arms. She spoke gently. "You were dreaming, my Lord. No one will harm the boys. Why should they?" He lay quietly for a while, listening to her soothing voice as she talked. "Once the coronation is over, perhaps we will have the boys to stay. King Edward is still a child; he will need time to adjust to his position as king. The responsibility is much to ask of such a young lad. We will have him here to play with our own son." Richard liked the idea. It was a grand idea in a fanciful world, but it could not happen now. The sadness filled his heart again. "Edward will not be crowned King." He spoke the words quietly.

Anne sat up, alarmed. "He will not? Why, my Lord, what has happened?" Richard left the bed and poured water from a jug. He sat beside her on the bed. He told her about his visit from Stillingham. Elizabeth's marriage was invalid. Edward was already married when he married her. Her children are bastards. She sat quietly and listened. His inner council wanted him to take the crown. If he did, the people would think he had usurped it. Yet, he could not stand by and let an illegitimate child take the throne. He feared for them. He was convinced there was plotting afoot.

Margaret, Countess of Richmond, was just waiting to sit her son on the throne. Edward had done the wrong thing, but he had put an end to the wars; he had brought about a stable government. He covered his face with his hands, "I fear the future, Anne, not for myself but for you, our son, and for Edward's boys".

The following morning, Richard visited the Tower. He was relieved to see both boys playing together with a ball. He asked after their health, and the young king admitted that he had suffered a great deal of pain in his jaw. "It is much better now since the new doctor gave me an herbal tincture. He said it is my third molar. It may give me trouble for some time." Richard nodded. "Did the Countess of Richmond attend with him?" The boy looked surprised. "Should I have expected her?" Richard shook his head. "No, no. Your mother had told her of your painful jaw, and she kindly offered to ask her own doctor, a very skilled man, to see if he could help. She asked for my approval, and of course, it was given." Edward thanked him and, turning, threw the ball at his brother. Richard was pleased to see them safe and apparently happy. He bid them farewell, then shuddered; the dream was still with him.

Richard had made up his mind. For the sake of England and Edward's boys and listening to his advisors, he would go along with their suggestions, but only so far. The preeminent men of the realm would be apprised of the secret, and their advice sought.

Hence the secret was relayed to an increasing circle of lords, prelates and gentlemen. Their response convinced Richard and his inner circle that it would be justified for young Edward to lose his crown to his uncle Richard, Duke of Gloucester.

The decision did not make Richard happy. Although he had endeavoured to do what was lawful and right, the images of the mutilated boys in the tower haunted him. He tried to tell himself that it was not his fault the boys were in such danger; it was the fault of Edward, their father. He was the one who had sinned against them, and also Eleanor and Elizabeth. He, in all truth, was not ambitious to become king. In some ways, it would have been a relief if he had unburdened himself of the truth about the pre-contract, and the people took it upon themselves to ignore it. Young Edward could have been crowned king, and he would have advised him the best he could but go back to ruling the north. However, he knew in his heart they would never have accepted an illegitimate boy to take the crown. The only hope had been that they did not believe it was the truth. If they offered him the crown as the only legitimate heir and he refused, who would take it? Buckingham? Henry Tudor? Wouldn't that destroy all the good work Edward and he had achieved for England?

He had allowed Buckingham freedom to present it to the people. Together they went with other magnates to hear the preacher Friar Ralph Shaa. His biblical text, "Bastard slips should not take root", shocked those who heard. The revelation of Edward's pre-contract meant that Elizabeth and Edward's marriage was invalid and 'the children begotten her were illegitimate.' The children of Clarence were disqualified by his attainder. Richard Gloucester was the heir of York and, therefore, rightful King of England. Buckingham had also ensured that a number of preachers declare the illegitimacy of the late King Edward. He was not the son of the Duke of York but was conceived in adultery. The Duke of Gloucester winced when he heard this. They had gone too far. True, it had been whispered before when the Duchess was informed of Edward's marriage to Elizabeth Woodville she became so enraged she claimed Edward was conceived in an act of adultery and, therefore, not worthy of the honour of kingship. She was prepared to swear, on oath, it was true. Those close to her believed it was her disappointment in Edward's actions. She wanted better for her son.

Richard had raved in anger when he was at home with Anne. "They had gone too far. It was an attack upon his house. It served no purpose." He thought about the hurt it would have caused his mother. Would she believe it came from him? Anne felt his pain. She knew this was just the beginning. There was no joy in being close to the crown. She remembered the awful months she was married to the Lancastrian Prince Edward of Wales. He was cruel and hateful. She was only 14 and had cried bitterly when her father had arranged the marriage. It meant leaving her Yorkist friends and family. She was regarded as a traitor, yet she had no say in the matter at all. When her husband, Prince Edward was killed, she was simultaneously terrified and ecstatic.

She smiled, recalling her happiness when Richard, the love of her life, had rescued her from the home of Isabel and Clarence. Isabel and Anne were heiresses to their parents' vast estates and Clarence, determined to keep the entire inheritance of the sisters, refused Richard's request to marry Anne. However, Richard had defied them all. He had rescued and married Anne under Clarence's very nose.

Anne looked at Richard. He was devastated to hear the scandalous rumours about his mother. How could anyone think he was unkind and ruthless? She knew differently.

"My Lord, how say you we stay with your mother for some time to give her support? That will not only make her happy but show the people the source of the evil rumours is not from you." Richard smiled and, walking over to her, took her in his arms. How comforting and sweet-natured she was. "I think it a marvellous idea. We will take our son with us. She would enjoy that. Clarences' children shall come too. He was always her favourite. I am not sure she will ever forgive my part in his death though she knows without a doubt that George brought it upon himself. Although I must admit that since hearing of Edward's secret marriage, I understand better why Edward was so determined he should be silenced. He could forgive him for his other acts of treason. But George would have undoubtedly used the knowledge against him, so anxious he was to get the crown." He was silent for a moment of reflection. He had no idea of the terrible secrets his brother had carried with him since becoming king. Could such a man have any happiness? If he delved deeper, what other things would he find that tortured Edward's soul? No wonder he died so young.

Chapter 16

Collingbourne stared at the document he held in his hand. He mumbled snatches of the message to himself, trying to make sense of it all. Edward was married when he married Elizabeth Woodville. Their marriage was, therefore, invalid - their begotten children, bastards. The late king's sons, Edward and Richard, are not eligible to inherit the throne. The Protectorate and council would value the advice of all lords, prelates and gentlemen. Was this a joke? But no, apparently, it was not. Buckingham's seal was clearly to be seen. He couldn't wait for Margaret to arrive as she had promised.

He wasn't surprised that Margaret already had knowledge of the content probably before he had received it. Stanley had trembled with excitement about the extraordinary secret that had been revealed to him at the inner council. He could not contain himself and spilt all to his wife that very evening. Margaret's calculating brain immediately considered the advantage this could be to her son's cause. Two more were removed from succession. Only Richard stood in the way. She dismissed Stanley's warning. He wanted none of her lofty ideas. She had been forbidden to start plotting on Henry's behalf. The council, particularly Buckingham, had been in favour of the Protectorate using the pre-contract to take the throne. It had been Richard who was cautious. He would only agree to move forward if advised to do so by the highest men of the realm. Margaret passed this unexpected news to Collingbourne.

"And where do you stand in all this?" Collingbourne appeared to be teasing, but he was interested in Margaret's view. She understood his tease was a pretence and was too clever to be caught to tell more than she wished.

"Why, William dear. I am merely a woman. You will have noticed that the letter you received only concerned the cream of society and that, of course, does not include women." He smiled, enjoying her game and answered.

"I didn't ask if you received a letter; you don't need one. I am quite certain you will have your say and make sure it gets to the ears that matter." She smiled sweetly.

"Perhaps you are right. The path to getting Henry on the throne is not straight; I am aware of that, there are unexpected twists and turns, but it will end in the right place. Let Richard take the throne. Henry will be two closer if Edward's boys are not eligible. More fool Edward I say. He must have known what he was doing if he married Elizabeth Woodville when he already had a wife. It was a foolish gamble. He probably thought he was in command of the situation, but clearly, he was not. One needs to be very astute or cunning to prevent truth from revealing herself. You cannot afford one error."

She gave him a kiss on the cheek. He offered her an ale or wine. She preferred the wine. Later when they sat in the evening sunshine, relaxing, she asked the question she had been keen to know the answer. "Did you know Edward was already married when he married Elizabeth? You were such good friends. I would be surprised if he didn't tell you." Collingbourne leaned back in his chair. It was a sensitive subject. It was a complete shock and had annoyed him intensely ever since he heard about it. At first, he had not believed it, and he was quick to defend Edward, but then, remembering things of the past, he realised it was the kind of thing Edward would do. It was a long time ago, but he remembered how smitten he had been with the lady he had met not long after he became king. He had confided he had met the most beautiful woman in the world, but when Edward asked for more, he shut up like a clamp. Not only did he go quiet, but he became agitated. Then his behaviour was strange for months. He appeared to be on top of the world but never had time for anyone. Collingbourne had thought it was just an affair that he enjoyed, but something was different. Then suddenly, his behaviour changed. He became moody and quick to temper. He refused to socialise, and for a while, Collingbourne thought he had offended him. Then unexpectantly, Edward came slapping him on the back and invited him for a drink or gave a warning that he would be at Ludgershall Castle for a hunt. It was then he became mixed up with his cousin Somerset and rumours were spread about the close relationship being something more than normal, even to the fact that Somerset shared his bedroom. His thoughts were interrupted by Margaret's voice. He started. "Where were you, William? You certainly were not with me."

"I beg your pardon, Margaret. Deep in thought so that I could answer your question. No, I was not aware of the fact, and I can tell you I was deeply upset when I heard about it. I thought there were no secrets between Edward and me. I believed Edward was honourable, but it appears he deceived us all, including Elizabeth. How humiliating this must be for her. It is totally beyond my understanding why he would do such a thing. What will become of his boys?"

"You believe it is true then?" Margaret almost whispered the words.

"It is difficult not to when a man of the cloth swears he conducted the marriage. What better evidence could you have than that?"

"You don't think it is Richard's own invention to usurp the crown?" Collingbourne flashed a look of anger. "I wouldn't believe it of Richard, no. I have spent hours in his company. I have never seen a trace of disloyalty to his brother or to England, for that matter. He has always been honest and fair in his dealings with people. I have known him since he was a young boy. He looked up to Edward, and admired everything he did. He was kind of heart. Why, when we found Clarence, his brother, guilty of high treason yet again, he was devastated. Edward insisted on the sentence of death. Although he accepted Edward's decision, I know he begged him to reconsider. No, Richard would not lie or deceive us in such a way as bribe Stillingham to tell the story."

Margaret could see how moved Collingbourne was. She had hoped to convince him that Richard was wicked, ambitious and would do anything to claim the crown. Clearly, although he was disappointed with Edward, he was not ready to change his allegiance yet.

Within days it became clear that there was sufficient support for Richard to be king. Richard was hesitant even when he heard that the Lords and Commons had recorded their unanimous approval that the Lord Protector should be offered the crown. Nevertheless, when he faced the great assemblage who had gathered beneath the battlement of Baynard's Castle and Buckingham read out the petition, he acceded, not quite sure whether it was pride that so many citizens of all classes had appealed to him to accept the crown or the fear of the consequence if he did not. If ever Richard had thought our destiny was chosen for us, it was now. He knew that most men believed he would take the throne, he had sensed it for weeks, some cynically, others angrily and even those who were hopeful, when indeed he had not the slightest thought of doing so. Did he ever really have a choice? Wasn't it true he was trying to justify a decision already made by the gods?

Anne was anxiously waiting for him as he moved towards the steps to obey the call to descend and ride with them to Westminster. "Was I right to accept? Will you be with me, Anne? "She placed a hand on his. "Yes, my Lord. You could do no other, and of course, I will always be by your side." She watched as he made his way down to the waiting crowd amid cheers of King Richard. He mounted his horse and rode ahead of the Lords, prelates and gentry to Westminster Hall. She should be happy for him, but her heart felt heavy. Unwanted intrusive thoughts crept into her mind. What did the future hold?

Collingbourne sat astride his horse, taking an evening ride

through the forest of Ludgershall. Recent events had shaken him. He recalled the occasions he had ridden with Edward in these same forests, particularly when he first became King. There was no other man like Edward. It seemed the gods had blessed him with every gift possible. His charisma charmed all who met him. His daring commanded respect, and life was seldom dull in his company. His temper could flare unexpectedly, and Collingbourne had learned to read the signs and avoid confrontation. Collingbourne recalled the times he had fought alongside him. He was a fearful opponent on the battlefield, and his prowess in warfare enabled him to become King of England. Who would have thought it would end like this? Disgraced, a liar and cheat.

His thoughts turned to the recent coronation of King Richard. How grand it had all been. Buckingham had usurped the position of the Duke of Norfolk to be first officer of the coronation, and the day before the coronation wearing his gown of blue velvet, no one outshone him. However, on the day, it was King Richard, in a gown of purple velvet, who walked with a bishop on either side of him to the Abbey who, was the centre of attention. Buckingham proudly carried his train. Collingbourne thought how ironic it was Margaret, Countess of Richmond, the mother of Henry Tudor, who held the Queen's train while the Duchess of Norfolk and numerous countesses took positions behind the queen. How was it she had been given the honour? He gave an amused laugh. What thoughts had been passing through her mind? He would give a King's ransom to know.

Collingbourne continued guiding his horse in a slow trot under the canopy of trees. Small patches of light filtered through the leaves, creating a mosaic of light and shadows. Birds called one to the other. He thought of Edward's boys in the Tower. How confused and frightened they must be. What will Richard do with them? Perhaps he would take responsibility for them at his castle as he had with Clarence's children. Richard had shown responsibility and kindness to them; he would do the same for Edward's boys

It was no life for them in the Tower. He had heard rumours that there were those who wished to free the boys. In fact, he had been invited to a meeting by Sir John Cheyney just days after the coronation. Cheyney, Master of the House to King Edward, had lost his position to Sir James Tyrell under the redistribution of offices by the new King. Others who had lost their office to new favourites of Richard were ready to rebel in some way.

Collingbourne sighed. He had understood that if Edward had indeed been married to Eleanor Talbot when he married Elizabeth, then it was of no fault of Richard that young Edward could not be crowned. Nor had Richard pushed to be king. He had allowed the people to decide what should be done, and they had begged him to take the crown. Why, then, couldn't everyone get on with life? He heard Margaret's words again spoken when they dined with Walter Hungerford. "What if Richard has played his cards very well? Edward has been discredited, and his son is not eligible for the crown. Who is left? A man who is a brilliant tactician who is evident by the strategies he adopts on the battlefield could be quite capable of playing all of us." Hungerford had looked sharply at Margaret. "Are you doubting him, my Lady? Margaret smiled but neither confirmed nor denied she was. He remembered his irritation that she had made a comment. Was it to be followed by a suggestion that Henry Tudor would do very nicely? He wondered if she had noticed his displeasure and decided to say no more.

Collingbourne had brought his wife and children to Ludgershall Castle for a change of scenery. He loved it there, and his wife had learned to love it too. The years had passed since King Edward had told him he needed an heir and arranged for the marriage of a young widow, also named Margaret. She brought her two boys from her previous marriage with her and had given him two daughters. He doubted there would be a son now, but he was not disappointed. Edward had been kind to him, and his daughters were a treasure.

Collingbourne had been careful about his relationship with the Countess. He had no wish to distress his wife. In his own way, he loved her and believed he was as good a husband as any man. Margaret, the Countess, had been a guest at their manor on several occasions, and since she owned Lydiad, where Collingbourne spent much of his time, his wife at no time questioned her visits. He never knew that his wife was quite aware of his close relationship with the Countess but chose to ignore it. She had lost the love of her life on the battlefield, fighting for King Edward and had been heartbroken. She never wanted to go through that pain again. So she lived with the happy memories of their time together and was grateful that her new husband had taken such care of her and been a good father to her boys. She was delighted with her beautiful daughters, and she knew William adored them. Yes, they were a happy family. William worked hard and received many rewards from the King. He had become very wealthy, collecting much property and was one of the most powerful gentlemen in Wiltshire. She was proud of him. There was no need to be concerned that he believed he loved the Countess. She had observed the Countess when she was with them. She was sure she did not return the love that Collingbourne believed they shared. William had told her that her son was Henry Tudor, and she was determined to see him crowned King of England. Margaret Collingbourne watched how the Countess played with his affection. The Countess knew William had the ear of the late King Edward, and for a lady who was so determined to get her son on the throne, Margaret wondered if that was his main attraction. She had realised years ago she didn't really like the Countess. She didn't believe she could be trusted. Her womanly intuition warned her that she was dangerous. She hoped and prayed that William wouldn't be influenced by her perilous schemes. Perhaps things would be different with Richard on the throne.

If it was hoped that once Richard was crowned, there would be stability, there must have been many who were disappointed. It began with movements in South England in the counties of Wiltshire, Sussex, Essex and Hampshire with a conspiracy to rescue Edward's daughters from the sanctuary. Reginald Bray, a faithful servant of the Countess of Richmond, was to communicate with the countess herself and afterwards with the Queen Dowager in the sanctuary. Unfortunately for the conspirators, Richard's spies at the Abbey had been instructed to watch the Queen Dowager carefully. It was learned that there was a plan to rescue the princesses. Richard had been prepared for such an act and had put John Nesfield, his faithful supporter, in command. No one was allowed to go in or come out of the sanctuary without his permission. Nesfield had suspected there was something afoot when unusual activities had occurred and sent his messenger to Richard warning him.

Richard cursed when he received the coded message. He was out of London and had already heard rumours of another plan to rescue the two princes. Since the terrible dream he had experienced, he had been concerned about his nephews' safety. He had plans. He would move them out of harm's way. It was true of all the places in England that the Tower was considered the safest place for them to be. But the thick walls and guards were only as safe as the men one could trust. As far as his nephews were concerned, the only man he trusted was himself. He had told no one, except his wife Anne, of his plan, but he needed to act hastily upon hearing the news of an attempted rescue. He set forth immediately to put his plan into action.

Buckingham was surprised to receive an urgent message from Sir Robert Brackenbury, the constable of the Tower, to ride in haste to the Tower. He gave no reason; the matter was too delicate, but he prayed Buckingham would heed his request. The puzzled Duke realised the matter must have been of importance and, thinking how fortunate it was that he was in London, began immediately to prepare for the visit. He arrived to find Brackenbury distraught; he could hardly pronounce the words as they tumbled from his mouth. "The Princes, they are both gone. Vanished into thin air!"

Buckingham stared at him. Had he drunk too much? Was he out of his wits? He spoke roughly.

"Pull yourself together, man! You make no sense. What do you mean 'vanished into thin air?"

The guard sat down. Buckingham saw tiny beads of perspiration begin to appear on his brow. He passed him a kerchief. Brackenbury mopped at his brow, then began again.

"When I took in their breakfast, they were nowhere to be seen. At first, I thought they were hiding for a laugh. I was not amused, I can tell you. I searched every area they could have been. Their beds were rumpled. Their clothes were untouched, and their favourite possessions were in place. It is a mystery. They have vanished.

The Duke stood for a few minutes, speechless. He began to feel clammy. How could it be possible? "Have you sent a message to the king?" He knew he was floundering, not knowing what to say.

Brackenbury shook his head. "I'm not sure where he is. I thought you, the most powerful man in the land after the king, you would know what to do." Buckingham would normally have enjoyed the flattery, but in this case, he wanted none of it. It was too hot to handle. He had heard there was a move to rescue Edward's boys from the Tower. Perhaps they had been successful. He cursed Brackenbury under his breath. His very presence in the Tower might throw suspicion on him. What if the princes had been murdered? He could be accused of committing the act under the king's instruction or, worse still, of his own volition. He could feel a rapid heartbeat and the need for air in his chest. He had to get out of the Tower quickly. Not sure of the last words he had mumbled to Brackenbury, he moved swiftly from the room, not breathing freely again until he reached fresh air.

Chapter 17

Buckingham had left abruptly, leaving the shaken guard unsure of what he was going to do. His first plan was to flee to Brecon Castle, where he could think. It would not do to be in London when the news broke. It was not certain from whom the news of the Princes' disappearance was learned. It spread like wildfire throughout London within hours, and soon, taverns were expressing their concern about their disappearance.

No sooner had the people expressed their shock and displeasure about the mystery of the young boys' disappearance when the rumour followed that they had been murdered. Immediately voices accused the King of being responsible. Who else had the motive to commit such a violent crime? There were calls for Richard to defend himself by presenting the Princes to the world. Richard had ignored their pleas.

Whispers were heard that it was the Duke of Buckingham who was guilty. He had access to the Tower and was seen there last week. Some argued King Richard persuaded him to commit the murder, while others disagreed. Buckingham was power-hungry like Warwick before him. Richard had a need to watch his back. Indeed such comments proved to be true.

King Richard had been kind to Buckingham. He had gorged him with honours, and Buckingham had climbed so high he was dizzy with the success he had so easily achieved. Richard had not questioned Buckingham's request to become jailor to John Morton, Bishop of Ely, never dreaming that Buckingham had a motive. The Duke was intrigued by the mind of the master plotter, and once captive in his castle, he hoped to befriend him and learn the skill or at least use that extraordinary mind for his own visions. He was totally unaware that the master plotter was adept at reading men like books and was proficient at manipulation. Morton soon learned that the Duke was easily motivated by flattery. Even before the death of the Princes in the Tower, Morton had him in his power, and he unconsciously revealed his dreams.

Buckingham found himself working with the Bishop to uncrown King Richard. Morton cleverly suggested that they send a messenger to Margaret, the Countess of Richmond, and had

Buckingham believing the idea came from him. Margaret was delighted that Morton had, at last, contacted her and sent Reynold Bray, her shrewd servant, to Wales. He divulged that an insurrection was already in motion in the southern counties, and the Countess had communicated with many Lancastrian friends. The wily bishop did not include the Duke in the plans he and Bray had made.

When Bray had left, Buckingham invited the Bishop to dine with him. No longer was the status of a prisoner, the Bishop free to move around the castle. He sat in the Duke's best chairs and drank his expensive wine. His face beamed with smiles. Buckingham was easy to play.

They had enjoyed a magnificent dinner. The Duke had instructed that one of his finest French wines be served. They were seated in the late afternoon sunshine, fully content.

Morton picked this moment to change Buckingham's ambition to be king. "There is no doubt, my Lord, no one is more deserving than yourself for the crown, but have you considered there is another who could have, well not a better claim, indeed no, but perhaps a better chance?" Buckingham frowned, then barked.

"Who in the name of our father could that be, Bishop?" Morton smiled. He was careful in choosing his words. "Why, Henry Tudor, your cousin." Buckingham's jaw dropped. Before he could say a word, Moreton had explained that Henry was unmarried and free to marry the late King Edward's eldest daughter Elizabeth. He hastily added, "The Countess of Richmond has many Lancastrian followers, they included leaders of the plot, which is well underway, but naturally, it all depends on yourself. You have the power to seat Henry on the throne easily, as you did King Richard if you had a mind to." Buckingham's vanity was tickled. To bestow a crown on two monarchs within a few months was delightfully tempting, although it was not the pinnacle of the dreams he had recently nursed. However, he had committed himself too far. Richard would never trust him again. He had seen it all with Clarence and Edward. There was only one way forward. He must work with Henry Tudor to crush Richard. Even as he agreed with Moreton's plan, he had his own. It wasn't the end of his dreams, just a different path. After all, he was the legitimate descendant of Thomas Woodstock. Henry Tudor was an illegitimate descendant of John of Gaunt. No better than Edward V. The end result would be the one with the greatest army behind him. He had no doubt that would be himself. He didn't intend to breathe a word of that to the Bishop of Ely. He had learned that it was wheels within wheels. Moreton's cunning had rubbed off on him. They shared their common aims, but neither mentioned their secret thoughts.

Moreton rubbed his hands together and smiled with satisfaction. He had succeeded in winning Buckingham to join with Henry Tudor, a wonderful feat completed with such ease. The Countess would be delighted. But there was still the problem of the Princes in the Tower. Despite the fact they had been illegitimized, it could easily be reversed. Death was the only solution to that problem, whether rumoured or factual, and there was no better person to blame than King Richard himself. Moreton had no hesitation that Buckingham could be very convincing on that score.

There was great excitement when the rebels of the south learned that the Duke of Buckingham had decided to lead them. True to form, he convinced them that King Richard had murdered the princes, his own flesh and blood, and for that reason, he could no longer find the stomach to be loyal to him. Hence, his decision to join their party. He would bring with him a large number of followers to support their cause.

Richard held his hands as if in prayer. He closed his eyes and sighed. He felt as if someone had kicked him hard in the stomach. It pained him. Harry Buckingham had defected. His chief ally and friend had betrayed him after all they had been through together. So soon after placing the crown on his head, he had written to Henry Tudor and offered his support to place the crown on his. Whatever could he be thinking?

He had heard that Buckingham had accused him of killing his nephews, a heinous crime indeed, but the Duke had witnessed on many occasions his loyalty to Edward's sons. He had never borne witness to anything but kindness and love for them. It hurt; it hurt badly that Buckingham could think of him in that way. Yes, the boys had disappeared, but there was no evidence they were murdered. To cast the blame on him had divided the country. He had undermined his authority and probably, most of all, had injured his ego. Could he have misjudged the man so badly?

No matter. Now was not the time to procrastinate or wallow in self-pity. London was threatened by the men of Kent and Surrey. Henry Tudor was primed to land on 18th October and join Buckingham, who, together with his mighty force, would attack him, the King who they believed would be totally unaware of his danger.

Had Buckingham learned nothing? Did he think he was a fool and would not find out from his numerous spies that a conspiracy was brewing? Only a buffoon would believe a conspiracy of such size could remain a secret. True, he had no army with him now, but there was no one more adept than he to resolve that in a hurry. Within hours he had issued commands to the council at Westminster to arrange for his army to meet at Leicester on October 10th and 11th. The Kings Household sent out urgent appeals to their followers. By the 15th of October, Richard had proclaimed Buckingham as a rebel.

Richard was lodging at the Angel Inn in Grantham while he waited for the dawn of the 18th. Viscount Lovell had gone to meet his men at Banbury the previous day. Richard left with the Earl of Northumberland and Thomas, Lord Stanley. Northumberland left the room, and Stanley stood looking out of the window. He turned when Richard spoke. "Are you with me, Thomas?"

Stanley gave a look of surprise.

"My liege, I find your question difficult to answer. I am here, am I not?" Richard gave a cynical laugh. "Don't play games, Thomas. You know what I am asking. The countess, your wife, is undoubtedly up to her neck in this conspiracy. Do you think I am unaware of the money she has sent abroad to her son to finance this charade? Don't you realise my spies have reported her attendance at meetings giving financial support? I have evidence of written communication she has with Buckingham, her cousin, of course, John Cheyney, Richard Guildford, and William Stoner. Lovell was fooled by him. She blatantly associates with them all. She is playing a dangerous game – treason, some would call it." He tutted and walked closer to Stanley, putting his face close and staring into his eyes. Then whispered, "Yes, I can see you are here in body. But what about your soul?" Stanley turned his face. He felt uncomfortable with Richard staring into the windows of his soul. It was true; he had no reason to have left Richard's side. Margaret had been infuriatingly impetuous. She seemed to have no sense of caution. He was with Richard because he was on the winning side. If that changed, the story would probably be different. Margaret had no idea how she, in taking such risks, had endangered not only her own safety but his as well. He was too close to the king to simply walk away, but in truth, his loyalty was to himself. Richard moved away and cursed.

"Forgive me, Thomas. Buckingham has broken my heart." He turned and, moving toward Stanley, lay a hand on his shoulder. "You cannot be responsible for what your wife thinks, but you can give her less freedom."

When he opened his campaign on 24th October, King Richard intended to come between the Duke of Buckingham and the rebels in the West Country and the counties in the south and then turn to face Buckingham believed to be the daunting head of the rebellion. It seemed, however, that the heavens had sided with King Richard. From the start, Buckingham had unexpectedly been harassed by chieftains of the Vaughan family who were jealous of his power in Wales. Little did Buckingham suspect that King Richard had employed the services of Sir Thomas Vaughan of Tretower and Humphrey Stafford. The Vaughan's cut off Buckingham's communications with Wales and followed them, raiding the lands of Brecknock Castle and eventually rifling the Castle itself.

Stafford occupied all the marches and systematically destroyed the bridges over the Severn. Mother nature, too, was against him. On the 17th of October, a storm of unusual violence broke out in West England. Rivers broke their banks and never heard of floods swept away houses, corn, and cattle. Hundreds were drowned, and very serious damage to shipping. Even children in their cradles were seen floating in the fields. Thanks to Stafford, the bridges of the Severn were destroyed. Buckingham's army, unable to move, ran out of provisions and complained of hunger. It was little wonder that the men who had been forced to join his army became disgruntled. But disheartened as he was, Buckingham headed to Gloucester. But his followers lost confidence and deserted him and returned home. Buckingham swore to himself. He felt no faith in the few who had stood by him. He knew of a person he could trust, Ralph Banaster, one of his retainers. While his men slept, he left them and struggled towards Banaster's house in Shropshire. Much later, in the early hours of the morning, he banged his fists on the door, anxious not to be seen. Banaster cautiously opened the door, wondering who could be calling at this hour. He stared at the bedraggled man standing there, unsteady on his feet. It took him minutes to recognise the Duke; he could hardly believe what he saw.

"Are you going to invite me in, Ralph? Banister took a step back to let him pass. Buckingham struggled to a nearby chair. Banaster observed his sunken cheeks and weariness. He asked for a drink. Bannister pulled himself together and poured a jug of ale.

The Duke drank greedily. How good it tasted. After draining the jug, he closed his eyes and licked his dry lips and, leaning back in the chair, closed his eyes.

Banaster stared at the man who was his master and now expected his loyalty. Buckingham was a wanted man. King Richard offered a generous reward for his capture. Lady Luck had delivered the Duke to his door. The reward he would receive was extremely high.

The Duke suddenly opened his eyes and spoke. "I'll reward thee well, young Ralph, for the refuge you give me now." Banaster nodded, alarmed that the duke had appeared to read his thoughts. Buckingham could be generous, but he was a proclaimed rebel likely to be caught and not in a position to reward anyone.

Buckingham felt safe now. He could relax. He was losing the battle, fighting sleep. A bird twittered, and another responded. His breathing slowed, and he began to snore, softly at first. Banaster watched, fascinated. He noted a twitch of his nose, then a huge breath followed by a loud snore. He was gone to the land of Nod. He sat for a few minutes struggling with the meaning of loyalty. Then he decided. He owed loyalty to King Richard. For minutes he stood and watched him. Then he stealthily moved to the door. Once out, he sent a young lad to fetch the sheriff as quickly as he could, offering him a reward if he brought him to his house just as he had been told. Everything had been planned prior to Buckingham's arrival. He called after the boy, "Tell him it is for the king."

Returning to the house, he saw to his relief the Duke was still sound asleep. His head had dropped to one side. Loud snores echoed through the house. Banister had no idea how long it would take before the sheriff arrived, hours, days? He prayed it would be soon. Already his heart beat faster in fear Buckingham would find out what he had done. What if the boy came back and said he couldn't find the sheriff? What would Buckingham do if he realised he had been betrayed by a man who owed him loyalty? Perhaps it wasn't worth the reward. Trembling, he began to pray. "If Lady Luck has called at his door with the gift of Buckingham, please make sure she stays until the Sheriff arrives."

Several hours later, Buckingham awoke. He could smell something delicious. A pot was simmering on the fire. Banaster's wife Ruth had cooked a healthy broth. She was surprised when her husband had woken her and told her of their visitor. Could it really be the Duke himself? Why had they been so honoured? There would be jealousy in the village about this. A real duke in the house. He didn't dare tell her the truth. The less she knew, the better. It was enough to allow her to fuss about providing a meal.

She smiled happily when she saw Buckingham was awake. Giving a deep curtsey that nearly off-balanced her, she asked if he was hungry. His stomach grumbled in reply. Turning to Banaster, she told him to show the Duke where he could wash. She had already wiped out the bowl and placed a clean towel and her scented soap for his use. Banaster had laughed at her. "Men don't use that fancy soap, Ruth." She had laughed. "You might not, but dukes do."

Buckingham's stomach growled again as Ruth served the soup in a bowl. He couldn't wait. Snatching a huge chunk of bread, he dipped it in the swirling bowl of meat and vegetables. He savoured the flavours. Surely this woman was a better cook than any other. He didn't need to be asked if he would like more. As he finished, a loud hammering was heard on the front door. Ruth stood up and, quite forgetting she had a duke in the house, yelled, "There is no need to knock the door down!" To her dismay, the door was flung open, and the Sheriff and his men stormed in, striding towards Buckingham. The Duke stood up, knocking his chair to the ground. Ruth screamed, and Banaster stood looking guilty. His prayer had been answered.

"King Richard will be pleased to see you." The Sheriff grabbed him as he spoke, and placed the point of a sword lightly at his throat. His hands were tied. He said nothing, but Banaster was haunted the rest of his life by the look the Duke gave him as he was marched to the door.

Buckingham was thrown in goal, waiting for the judgement of King Richard. Much later, Buckingham learned that the mighty storm had prevented Henry Tudor's fleet from successfully crossing the Channel. Many ships were driven back, and only the

Earl's succeeded in getting across. To his displeasure, Tudor found that contrary to expectations, the coast was well guarded, and he was forced to move westward, landing at Plymouth. A welcoming group of country people was waiting on the shores to greet him. Tudor, suspicious, sent to ask whose troops they were but was not deceived by the answer that it was the Duke of Buckingham's forces. Now was not the time to embark. He set sail to return across the Channel.

The Countess of Richmond sat quietly at home, waiting for news of the rebellion. Collingbourne joined her. Although he was not directly involved, he knew about it. How could he not? Margaret was free to do as she wished with her husband away with the King. It had been a hub of excitement. He had heard snippets of plans in which Margaret was involved. She had tried to rope him in, but until the memorable day, he showed little interest. He remembered the occasion so well.

Margaret had persuaded him to accompany her to a banquet held at Buckingham's lavish great hall at Thornbury Castle, where a huge table had been set for dinner. He was so impressed with the place—the walls were built from large slabs of stone. Beams soared to the ceiling, and large led light windows displaying magnificent works of art added beauty. Above the huge stone fireplace was evidence of hunting carried out on the hundreds of acres that surrounded the castle. Huge antlers rising high above the head of deer looked down at the assembly.

Buckingham was in high spirits. There were several Lancastrians seated at the table, including Sir John Cheyney, Edward and Peter Courtney, Lionel the Bishop of Salisbury, and Sir William Stoner. He knew them all.

Margaret had taken his arm and, addressing John Morton, Bishop of Ely, said, "this is my dear friend William Collingbourne." He remembered his surprise. It was his understanding that Morton was under lock and key, not treated as a favoured guest.

Smiling, he recalled the young boys in their tights and tunics displaying the Buckingham coat of arms, who carried platters piled with food. Musicians heralded each course to the table. After dinner, the ladies strolled in the garden. The men had retired to another grand hall for their drinks and talks. Only now he realised it was a setup. Margaret wanted him included in a very important meeting of men who were conspirators of her plotting to get her son Henry on the throne of England.

"It's true then," Sir John had said, opening the topic to be discussed. "The young princes have been put to death. Was it Richard's doing?"

"I have no evidence," Buckingham began. "But when King

Richard heard about the movement in the south to rescue the princes, he angrily shouted they would soon be out of reach. I knew then he meant to have them murdered."

"Well, you're his confidant," Courtney spat. "Didn't he tell you how he intended to do that?

"Not at all," Buckingham answered coolly. "I think he sensed I was against it. In fact, I was mortified. Those words were the seeds of my disillusionment of him as King." Buckingham's eyes narrowed. Collingbourne recollected the way he looked around to see the effect of his words.

Morton spoke for the first time. "The arrogant pig is losing support. There's growing hostility towards him."

Collingbourne recalled he couldn't resist the temptation to speak. He raised his voice. "It's no wonder! Every day Richard strips someone in the south of his office and grants it to one of his men from the north." He was still hurting from the loss of his office to Duchess Cecily that Richard had bestowed on Lovell. Richard was just a boy when King Edward had placed him under guidance of Collingbourne to work on various commissions together. "Take heed of what Collingbourne can teach you. There's not much that'll get pass his eye." Richard had appreciated the advice he had offered him. Duchess Cecily had expressed her disappointment that her son had made the decision to give the stewardship to Lovell. She had thanked him for the excellent work he had done over the years and said she couldn't understand what Richard's motives were to give the stewardship to Lovell, but she had little say in the matter. Perhaps he should have confronted Richard.

"He doesn't trust the magnates in the south," Buckingham was speaking. "He knows there is still too much support for young Edward and opposition to him."

"And what about you?" asked Courtney. "You've made it damn clear where your support lies." He had scowled.

"Well, that was in the past," Bishop Ely had replied. "The duke has seen the error of his way and has decided to join forces with us." He beamed at Buckingham. Silence followed looks of disbelief. Courtney moved forward and offered his hand to Buckingham. "It'll be an honour to have you on our side." Buckingham accepted his hand.

"And not just to join forces," added Morton jubilantly. "The Duke has agreed to lead us in overthrowing Richard and bring Henry Tudor to the throne."

A few days later, still confused about Buckingham, Collingbourne visited Margaret again. The air was filled with the heavy scent of roses. The countess was sitting on her couch. She had already poured two goblets of wine and placed them on a heavy timber table beside her. She offered him the wine and, patting the cushion beside, invited him to sit. "Now, my dear,"

Collingbourne said, smiling. He brushed her lips with a kiss, took the goblet of wine, and sat down. "I know that look. What is it you are after?"

She gave a dazzling smile, took a sip of her wine, and then began. "Have you heard the news that King Richard has had the princes murdered?" Collingbourne looked surprised. It was not the conversation he expected.

"Don't look so surprised, dear." She lowered her eyes.

"Well, yes, I have heard rumours. Buckingham spoke of it at the banquet. They are only rumours."

They were distracted by two birds chirping excitedly over a worm.

"I am sure it is true. My source is very reliable. Richard sent one of his men and paid him well. He was concerned that attempts were being made to rescue the princes." William stared at her. He was sure her reliable source was her husband. All colour drained from his face. It contorted with pain as he struggled to come to terms with what he had heard.

"That swine!" His voice broke as he spoke. "They were so young, so innocent. How could he? His own flesh and blood! His own brother's sons."

He looked away, trying to conceal tears.

"They were a threat to his throne," the countess said without emotion.

He stood and began pacing the room. Turning, he said hoarsely. "Does Stanley know?" He searched her face for an answer. "Of course he does. He is your reliable source. How can Stanley bear to serve him?"

"He doesn't really have much choice, does he," she answered coolly. "Richard is demanding and has threatened him already with his son's life if he shows any sign of disloyalty," Collingbourne said nothing.

"I have a plan," the countess whispered. He looked up.

"Revenge?" he asked bitterly. "That won't bring back the princes."

"Not just revenge," she smiled sweetly and took his hand. "We cannot restore young King Edward to the throne, that is true, but we can remove King Richard from a throne he has usurped."

"Your son again. He hasn't a chance. Princess Elizabeth has a greater claim."

"I, too, believe Elizabeth should be queen, but Henry is young and a bachelor. If Henry married the princess, the rival houses of York and Lancaster would, at last, be united."

Collingbourne stared. The idea overwhelmed him. "What a daring plan." His voice was a whisper. "It's brilliant. Hostile factions could unite to put them on the throne together, and everyone would be happy. I'd still be loyal to Edward by helping his daughter to the throne. Will the Queen Dowager agree?

The countess smiled, amused that men were so naïve.

Collingbourne agreed it would be a solution, but now his anger rose against Richard and his violence towards the boys. No longer able to be still, he strode angrily from the garden room, waving off his man holding his horse. He called over his shoulder; he would walk for a while. "Bring him to me later," he barked.

Margaret watched him go and smiled. His anger pleased her. She had won.

He stormed over the fields venting his fury. An owl flew out from a tree, hooting loudly. Another responded from a nearby tree.

"Whose idea was it to get rid of the princes? Catesby? Ratliffe? Lovell? I bet they were all responsible. All feeding from the trough. They knew if young Edward was freed, their troughs would soon be empty. Animals! The lot of them! Curse of them all." He gave a sardonic laugh. "Cat…Rat…Dog…and HOG!"

William let out a primeval howl that echoed throughout the valley. Birds, roosting for the night, screeched and fluttered their wings in protest.

In the small hours of the morning, a man stood in the mist, hammering a note on the door of St. Paul's Cathedral. He stood back to admire his handiwork.

> *The Cat, the Rat, and Lovell, the dog*
> *Do rule all England under a hog*

He let out a soft, disdainful chuckle. Turned and walked away without a backward glance.

Chapter 18

William sat with the captured Duke of Buckingham. It was Saturday 1st of November.

Collingbourne had been allowed to speak to him. William's face filled with horror when he saw the state of Buckingham. He had become a babbling terror-stricken man who had lost his dignity.

"Make him see me, William," he pleaded, tugging at William's cloak. "I have information I will gladly give if he will save my life." He was almost in tears.

"I don't think anything you could offer would save you now." Collingbourne's stomach churned. He was deeply disturbed by the condition of the Duke. How fragile and fickle life could be. Just months ago, the Duke was a proud man of wealth and one of the most powerful men of the land. Who would have believed he could have been reduced to this?

"That witch…I begged her to come and help me, but she hasn't."

Collingbourne stared at the Duke. The witch? Surely he wasn't talking about Margaret. His gaze turned to the low thin bed with a mattress and dirty-looking hide. A tray of untouched food had been placed on a low wooden stall. It consisted of a watery broth and some kind of grey-looking meal. His stomach churned again. There was no toilet facility. The Duke was stained with urine. The stench was terrible.

"It was her, you know. She's the evil one. Pretends to be so close to God. A she-devil. That's what she is. She talked me into doing it. Be warned, William. She'll do anything for that son of hers." Collingbourne looked at him disdainfully but said nothing.

"Oh, I know you are sweet on her. Many men are. But if the King knew she was the one who murdered his nephews…" His eyes looked wildly at the door. "That would be the end of her."

Collingbourne screwed his face. He clenched his fists. He wanted to punch Buckingham, but the sight of his anguish prevented him. Buckingham sneered.

"You don't believe me, do you? What have I got to lose now

by lying?"

"You've a great deal to gain if the King believed you." He was thankful Richard wouldn't see him.

"I tell you, she and Moreton had the princes poisoned. Edward had a toothache, and his doctor called on him to relieve him of his pain. They poisoned both of them. I heard them talking of it."

"Are you telling me you stood by and let it happen?" Collingbourne turned white. He stood up and sat down again.

"I was too late and in too deep to do anything about it. She bribed Banaster to turn me in. She wants me out of the way now; I am no use to her. She's scared in case I talk. She's ruthless and will show no loyalty to you over her son."

Collingbourne was angry. Why was Buckingham making such claims? "How do you know she bribed Banaster?" He could hardly pronounce the words.

"He came to see me. Broke down," Buckingham looked Collingbourne straight in the eye. "He said he deeply regretted his actions." The Duke's voice was bitter. "She tempted him with huge offers of land and money. Banaster said she was ready to pay any amount to get rid of me. She claimed I had failed her. She couldn't see it was not my fault. Richard was smart. He had paid men to put every obstacle in my way. I heard they have rifled my castle, stolen and smashed every room. But it was the weather that beat me. We were trapped. Richard's men had destroyed all the bridges, and the Severn had broken its banks. We were low on supplies. The men, too hungry and cold, deserted. It wasn't my fault. There's no way Henry could have crossed the channel in that weather, and if he did, he couldn't have got to shore. But she blames me. Says I am incompetent and has no more use for me. She's done for me, William. My only hope is that Richard will give me an audience. I can tell him what she is up to. Will you ask the King to see me? I know you have his ear."

Collingbourne heard the words repeatedly singing in his ears. The Countess a murderer! It couldn't be true, but he knew it could. He had known and loved her for years. He, of all people, knew she would stoop to any level to get her son on the throne and save him from perceived danger.

"I'll do my best," was all he could find to say. Buckingham looked at him. His eyes were sunken. He knew he didn't have a chance. He was right. The wound he had given Richard was too deep. He couldn't bear to even look at his once close friend. The following morning, Henry Stafford, second Duke of Buckingham, was beheaded as a traitor on the newly erected scaffold in the marketplace of Salisbury.

Later in the week, Collingbourne visited Margaret. She was pale, and although appeared strong, she was fearful. She told William that Richard had assumed or chosen to believe that her husband had no part in the rebellion. He realised Lord Stanley was too powerful to offend. She dabbed her eyes with a kerchief.

"A special Act of Parliament has been passed against me that states I have conspired against King Richard and committed high treason. He has taken everything – my titles and land." She sobbed. "All given to Stanley to enjoy his lifetime and the punishment of attainder remitted. At his death, they go to the crown." She put her hand to her head. There was no mention that Richard had instructed Stanley to keep his wife in order. She didn't choose to tell Collingbourne that.

Margaret ceased the tears. William did not tell her his thoughts. She was lucky to be alive. He thought of Buckingham.

"I visited Buckingham," William watched her face intently. He made no move to take her hand or give her comfort. She looked startled, then gained her composure and asked how he fared.

"He was distraught. The King refused to see him." William paused, watching her. "He claimed you also deserted him." He kept his eyes on her face. "They beheaded him on Sunday."

She looked away, saying nothing. Collingbourne continued.

"He said he had something of particular interest to tell the King." She flashed a look of concern.

"Did he elaborate?" she whispered, blood drained from her face.

William knew she was guilty. He wasn't quite sure of what she was guilty of—murdering the princes or betraying Buckingham after she had persuaded him to betray Richard. He had been part of her life for many years, and understood there was nothing more important to her than her son's safety and her determination to see him on the throne of England. She was a strong woman who would let nothing prevent her from succeeding in her son's cause. However, he said nothing. He looked drained, empty. Rising to his feet, he gave her a gentle kiss on the cheek.

"No, my dear, he didn't. Nor did I wish to know." He smiled wearily and left the house.

King Richard's way of dealing out punishment was similar to that of his brother Edward IV. He spared the ordinary folk and never harassed them or imposed heavy fines. He was surprisingly lenient to those who were involved in the rebellion. He had as little as ten people executed. It was Buckingham who had given him the most grief. He would have staked his life on believing him to be loyal no matter what. Despite the entreaties he had received from many to at least give Buckingham an interview and hear what he had to say, Richard was resolved not to see him. It was not that he didn't trust Buckingham; he didn't trust himself. He ordered the execution on Sunday, ignoring the fact it was All Soul's Day.

The king was pleased to be at home with Anne. It concerned him that their son Edward had not been well. The doctors appeared to have no idea what was wrong.

It was late autumn, and the leaves had begun to fall from the trees. The evenings were already chilly, and Richard had insisted the fires be lit. He enjoyed the firelight in the darkened room, the smell of burning wood, and red glow after the flames died down. He tried to push all matters of state out of his head, but it wasn't easy. There was always something niggling in the back of his mind. Tonight it was the Queen Dowager. He knew she had been one of the conspirators of Buckingham's rebellion, but how could she be punished? Wasn't it enough she had lost her sons, and her children had been labelled illegitimate after all these years? He felt sorry for her. He knew she had no love for him and had understood that too. She believed he was her enemy, but she was wrong. Oh, so wrong!

It concerned him that she remained locked in the sanctuary with her daughters. There must be some way he could persuade her to free herself. He promised himself he would visit her and try again. It would give him much pleasure to see her daughters at his court this Christmas.

"I wish there was a way I could convince Elizabeth that I am not her enemy." He spoke his thoughts aloud, but they were for Anne's hearing.

"Perhaps there is." Her voice was soft. He looked over at her, wondering what she was thinking.

"She is a very unhappy woman. There are no certainties for her. She has lost so much. You have the power to give her hope." Richard put his hand to his chin. He knew what Anne was thinking. They had discussed the matter several times when they had time together. The rebellion had prevented action. Now it was over; he had to implement his plan. "My concern is she will not be able to keep her side of the bargain." Anne walked over and knelt at his feet. Taking his hands and looking directly into his eyes, she spoke. "My Lord. You are giving her an opportunity that she wouldn't have dreamed possible. You have to trust her. If she betrays that trust, it will be between her and her conscience." He bent and kissed her on her forehead. "I love you, Anne, better than anyone else in the world." She laughed. "I hope so. You would be in trouble if you didn't."

The following morning Richard sent a message to Elizabeth stating he intended to visit her at noon. He would be very happy if she would receive him. She read the message and sighed. No doubt it was about the part she played in Buckingham's rebellion. She had been expecting it. There was no use in refusing him; better to know her fate.

Richard arrived promptly. He was invited into her room. She curtseyed. He was alone. Two or three ladies sat discreetly behind her, engaged in needlework of one kind or another.

"Dismiss them." He spoke kindly. She waved a hand, and they

removed themselves.

They sat silently for a few moments. He noticed folds in her face and tiny wrinkles around her eyes. She had aged since Edward's death.

"Your majesty is well?" She asked the question with genuine concern.

"My lady, it concerns me that you continue to stay in the sanctuary when you must know you are in no danger. It would please the queen and me to see you and your daughters at our court this Christmas. The season is, after all, a time for family."

"Family? Whose family? I understand we no longer belong to the family of York. In fact, I hear that you are the one who has murdered my boys."

"Your boys have not been murdered." She forced a laugh, but it sounded strained. "Well, produce them!"

Richard leaned back in his chair. "And if I did, do you think they would be safe? It is not my fault that Edward did the wrong thing by you. I know you trust the Countess, Henry Tudor's mother, but you can't, you know. If I produced the boys, do you think they would have a chance to live? I don't think you are such a fool as that. Their only hope of living is to be as far away as possible from London."

Elizabeth stared at Richard. "Margaret is my friend. She wants

Henry to marry Elizabeth and make her Queen." Richard shook his head. "And why do you think she wants that? Simply to put her son on the throne! Elizabeth has more right to the throne than Henry Tudor. Do you really think she or Henry would allow your sons to live? Why do you think I have removed them from the Tower?

Elizabeth was confused. Was Richard speaking the truth? Were her dear boys really alive? Tears welled in her eyes. What was she to believe? Perhaps Richard was right. Margaret was dedicated to seeing Henry on the throne, and marrying her daughter Elizabeth made it seem possible for him to achieve it.

The king watched her face while she tried to cope with what she was hearing. "But you," she whispered. "You are on the throne. There is no place for Elizabeth even if what you say is true." He sighed. "Isn't that what this whole rebellion has been about? You, the countess, and a dozen others planned that I wouldn't be on the throne much longer." He laughed. "But you failed. I didn't even need to strike a blow." He changed his tone. "I am offering you the opportunity to allow your sons to live and enjoy their life elsewhere. I have pardoned your older son, Thomas Grey, as much as he offended me. You can tell him he can come back to England if he chooses.

"And you will return his properties?" Elizabeth asked anxiously.

"Not entirely. He will pay that price. I have other plans for that parcel of land, but Thomas will be compensated." Elizabeth didn't argue but waited for Richard to continue.

"Your son Edward will live in a secret location far away, safe as long as he remains there. He has been given a new identity and property to live peacefully for the rest of his life. If he tries to come back, I cannot guarantee his life will be safe."

Elizabeth sat silently. She asked about her younger son Richard. Was he alive too? Richard nodded. He is safe but has been taken to a different place, and he, too, has been given a new name. It is too risky for them to be together." She didn't protest; she knew it was true.

"Elizabeth. You must work with me to save your sons' life. If you tell anyone they live, you may just as well kill them yourself. In time, things may change, but for now, it is crucial they are believed dead. You must tell no one, not even your daughters.

It is my wish that you release the princesses and encourage them to attend court. I will not insist. You have to trust me. You also. Give yourself a life."

"Why are you doing this, Richard?"

"Would you believe I loved my brother Edward and I love my nephews? Illegitimate or not, they are my brother's children. He was a damn fool for what he did. I know you don't trust me, but you have no reason to fear me. If you tell anyone, I have the boys, I will deny it.

"How can I be sure they are alive?" Richard sighed. "What did I say about trust? Elizabeth tightened her lips. Richard leaned forward.

If you agree to my request, you can visit your son. I will arrange it with a man I trust with my life. If I do that, can you trust yourself to keep silent?" He began to stand. He had done all he could. Was she convinced? He didn't know. Would she cooperate? He didn't know that either. Would he be a fool to trust her? Possibly, but it is a risk he would have to take. Surely she would not betray her own son.

He turned to go. "Richard, and my punishment. You haven't told me how I should be punished? Am I to lose my property and money? Perhaps I deserve it." He smiled. "I think you have been punished enough, Elizabeth. It is not for me to make your life more difficult than it is. But heed what I say. You may not easily be rid of Margaret, but watch her like a hawk. She cannot be trusted, particularly when it involves her son Henry." He left the room.

She sat quietly, not calling her women at all. Perhaps Richard was right. She would send her daughters to court. How happy that would make them. As for herself, she was not sure of that yet. Suddenly life felt so much better. Her boys were alive. She couldn't see them. She mustn't tell anyone. She felt like shouting it to the world. How would she manage to keep a secret like that? But she must. She must. She felt sure that one day she would see them again. Every bone in her body believed they were alive. It had to be true. Then it struck her what a sacrifice Richard was making. Many believed he had murdered them. They had called for him to show them if he was innocent. But he would not. He took the blame to save their lives. Men who once were his friends had turned against him. They would have killed him if they could. She thought of Buckingham. He had turned against Richard because he thought he had murdered the boys. He said he had proof. But it was a lie. Margaret and Bishop Ely had encouraged him. They, too, said they had proof. Was Richard right about Margaret? She thought it was kindness, which made her suggest she allow Henry Tudor to marry her daughter. Now she could see it was to benefit her son, not her or Elizabeth. To carry out their plans, they had to denounce Richard and push him off the throne. Why hadn't she seen it before? Edward had always warned her of Margaret. When Buckingham failed to get Henry on the throne, she deserted him. More than that. She set out to deliberately get rid of him. She knew Margaret had guessed Buckingham was on his way to Banaster for protection. She had made sure Banaster had been persuaded by a very generous offer of property and income. When Buckingham turned up, he invited him in and told the boy who would be hanging around to call the Sheriff of Shropshire. Even the Sheriff had been warned to expect notification and stay around the area. Richard was right. It would be foolish to let her know her sons were alive. She would follow Richard's advice, be wary of Margaret, and keep the secret too.

She hastily sent a message to her son Thomas, Marquess of Dorset, to abandon Henry, Richard had pardoned him, and he was welcome home. She made it known to Richard that she would surrender her daughters into his care. But what of her daughter Elizabeth? Did she do the right thing in allowing Margaret to persuade her to agree to the union between Elizabeth and her son Henry? Would it bring peace? Henry was not King of England yet, and maybe he never would be. Time would tell. She would bide her time.

Chapter 19

Margaret blamed Buckingham they had lost this time, but she was not beaten. She hurriedly sent messages to Henry, assuring him that all was not lost. It was unfortunate that such unexpected storms hindered their progress. Richard had been lucky. Buckingham was a fool, but there was no need to worry about him. Richard had dealt with that. She did not tell him about her own financial losses. It infuriated her that Richard had stolen all that was hers; even if he had given it to Thomas, there was no easy access for her to use it. Thomas was reluctant to involve himself in her efforts to sit her son on the throne despite not being totally opposed to the idea. He liked to be on the winning side. She knew it had nothing to do with loyalty. It didn't take her long to contact

Reynold Bray to start raising money for her son. Next time they would be successful.

Collingbourne was the thorn in her side now. He knew too much and was dangerous. She had no understanding of his idea of loyalty and felt threatened. She walked around her bedroom, wringing her hands, talking to herself.

"He's much too in love to betray me, but he's been a faithful Yorkist and very loyal to Edward. If he finds I have deceived him about the death of the princes, will he still remain loyal to me? I can't take the chance and risk the success of dear Henry."

She began spreading the news that it was Collingbourne who had pinned the seditious doggerel on the door of St. Paul's. He hadn't told her himself, but of course, she was aware of the fact. When he stormed off that night, she had him followed and watched. It had amused her at the time, but although humorous, it was a foolish thing to do. Margaret was conscious of the fact it wasn't just his reaction to hearing that Richard was guilty of murdering the princes that had resulted in him writing the verse; he had been nursing the injury received when Richard had given his position of Steward to Duchess Cecily, Richard's mother, to Lovell. She believed it was a matter of ego. He didn't need the position. He was wealthy enough. She had made certain that Richard's spies were aware that Collingbourne had attended meetings with the rebels and passed the information to the king.

Despite his knowledge that Collingbourne attended the meetings, Richard found no evidence he was involved or that he had committed himself. He wasn't convinced that Collingbourne had betrayed him. Collingbourne had always been loyal to Edward, who was a good friend. Further, he had worked alongside him and brother Clarence on various commissions. Nevertheless, he was in the clutches of the Countess. Who knows what evil influence she had!

Months passed by. People had lost interest in who wrote the ditty and pinned it to the doors of St. Paul's. Cathedral. She had not seen Collingbourne for several months. Her spies told her he had been very busy on various commissions. Margaret too, had been busy.

Eventually, the king issued a writ for Collingbourne's arrest. Margaret was delighted but not satisfied it would be sufficient to keep him silent she began more rumours. It was alleged Collingbourne was one of the secret agents in the first revolt against Richard's authority. He not only corresponded with Henry Tudor but also tried to involve Lois XI in the plot. This was a serious act of high treason, resulting in royal officers beginning their hunt for him.

Walter Hungerford had heard the rumours and had a very good idea about who was responsible for spreading them. He knew Collingbourne was at Lydiad and made his way to visit him.

William greeted his friend warmly. Walter had hardly entered the hall when he began to speak.

"You are no longer safe, William, my friend, and it disappoints me to tell you that your enemy is Margaret, who you believed was your friend." Collingbourne said nothing. Walter had expected anger, maybe disbelief. He began again.

"My friend. Surely you have heard the rumours that you have been in contact with Louis XI and Henry Tudor? That is high treason, William."

"Of which I am not guilty." Collingbourne insisted. "Richard will not believe that."

"Don't be a fool, William. These rumours were whispered into Richard's ear by no other than Stanley himself. And who has the ear of Stanley? William blanched. He knew it was true. He had expected it. Margaret was scared. She felt cornered. She did not trust him enough to believe he would never betray her. He felt the tears as they began to well up in his eyes. Soon they tumbled down his cheeks. He hung his head, ashamed that he had no control over his emotions.

Walter allowed him to cry. He moved to the side table and poured two drinks. Without speaking, he handed one to William. He sat waiting, slowly sipping his own while the bond of friendship tied them closer than ever.

Finally, Walter spoke. "You must hide, William. Give Richard time to cool. I have places you can go."

"I have no desire to run. Let them take me if they must. It is late, my friend, and I am tired and intend to retire for the night. You should be home. I am grateful for your support. Walter noticed the deep lines in William's face. He did look tired, but he was such a stubborn man. He was in danger. Once Richard's men found him, there would be no mercy. He tried again to persuade his friend to go into hiding to save his life.

"Collingbourne, don't be such a stubborn ass. If you will not save yourself, think of your wife Margaret and your children. Come with me. I will inform your family but keep your whereabouts from them. Then they will be safe too.

Collingbourne weakened. "Well, come for me later. There is a matter I must attend to first."

Once Walter had gone, William sat down at his desk, picked up his quill feather, and began to write:

My Dearest Margaret,

I send these words to comfort you in these dark hours. I feel deeply the torment you must be suffering, but that is nothing new for you. Men have fallen around you since childhood, and you have lost so many of those you love. These are dangerous times, dear one, but you, more than anyone are aware of that.

You have fought for Henry's safety all your life, and I know there is nothing you wouldn't do to keep him safe – even risk damnation and hell. You have the strength of a lion, dearest. What strength and foresight you showed when you sent him to exile, never knowing when he would return! Such is your passion for him. I could never compete.

However, although I cannot condone what you have done, it is not for me to pass judgement. God will do that. I can only give you my word, dearest, that I will not betray you. Your secret will go with me to my grave. Tears come to my manly eyes when I think that after all our years of love together, you didn't have enough trust in me to know that your secret would be safe, however much I deplored your actions. Margaret, the disappointment and your lack of faith in me have broken my heart. There is nothing Richard can do that could cause the pain you have inflicted on me!

I know the words that have reached Richard have come from your own sweet lips, and you knew they were lies and exactly what the consequence of such words meant.

It is our downfall that we men underestimate the power and wit of women.

What fools we are. Nevertheless, I remember you in my prayers and forgive you.

Farewell, my dearest. I am sure you will succeed in your dreams for Henry. Who would dare to doubt you?

Love forever in this world and the next.

Will

He carefully pressed his seal on the letter and, calling his servant, instructed him to take it to the Countess of Richmond without delay. Then he sat and began another letter.

My darling Margaret,

When you hold this letter in your hands, I will be far away, and you may have heard King Richard is after my blood. Do I deserve this? I do not believe so.

I cannot blame Richard; he is as innocent as I am. Lies and deceit make us do things that we would not dream of under normal circumstances. But these are not normal times. There are those who seek power and will do anything to achieve it.

I have no doubt that the King's men will find me, and to be honest, in some ways, I hope they do. I would dearly love to prove my innocence, but I am fully aware that the law is a fool. Those who judge me, my enemies, will believe what they want to believe. They will distort the truth in such a way it is not recognisable.

My heart is torn when I realise what I have done to you and our children. I wish I could obliterate the past. I have loved and trusted in one who I know has betrayed me. Yet, I can do nothing but accept the injustice because I cannot save myself by betraying her to prove my innocence. I can only apologise to you for my weakness. Yet, some would call it strength.

Thank you for being my wonderful wife. Thank you for my children. I have arranged some finances with Walter to make sure you live comfortably because I fear the King may take all I have. I hope and pray that you will not suffer too much and that one day Richard will learn the truth and pardon me.

Margaret, perhaps I have not always shown you the love I have for you. I realise you have patiently shared me with the Countess, believing I was not aware of your knowledge of the relationship. I was, my dear, but I didn't know how to explain that my loving her did not mean I did not love you. Please believe me when I say you have enriched my life.

Love to you and the children.

William.

He then gathered a few belongings and waited for Walter.

The messenger arrived at Margaret's manor. Unfortunately, Lord Stanley was home and, careful to follow the king's command, insisted that the messenger give him the letter. He promised he would ensure the countess received it.

He kept his word and took the letter immediately to his wife. Margaret blushed when she recognized Collingbourne's seal and, fumbling, tried to slip the letter into her bodice. Stanley stood, watching her.

"Aren't you going to read it?" Stanley asked, keeping his eyes fixed on her. Flustered, she muttered something about later. She had a headache. It was not important.

"My lady, I insist you read it now." Lord Stanley spoke kindly but was firm. Margaret had no option.

She read the letter, and tears began to fill her eyes. Lord Stanley gently took the letter from her hands and began reading. Coldly he demanded an explanation. Margaret rose from her chair, walked around the room, and sat down again. Clearly, she didn't know what to say. She fiddled with her belt, with no intention of confessing all to her Lord. She was too wise for that. She decided to resort to womanly power and collapsed into tears.

"I cannot tell you, my Lord," she sobbed. "I wish not to implicate you and cause you danger with the King."

"Fiddlesticks Margaret! The king is no fool. He knows what you're up to. Hasn't he proved that already?"

"Yes, my Lord." She wiped her eyes and looked at him demurely. "But it is because he believes you were not involved; he spared your life and showed compassion to me." She raised her eyes to see what impact her words had.

Stanley was not easily fooled. He strode up and down the room, glowering. "You know as well as I do that it is politics. Richard knows damn well I have resources that could embarrass him, and he can't afford to take risks. It's a cat-and-mouse game.

He knows I give you all the damn support I can." He stormed around the room, trying to contain his anger. Then he began again.

"Was he your lover?"

Margaret dropped her eyes but said nothing.

"Damnation, my lady, don't you think I have feelings?" He stared at her again, and they both remained silent for a few minutes. "Well, I guess you don't," he snorted. "You'd better tell me what he is on about Margaret. How can I protect you if I don't know what you're up to?" He walked over to her and sat down.

"He arranged contact with Henry," she said quietly.

"I'm not interested in what he's done!" stormed Stanley. He got up and strode about the room again. "It's what you have done! Damn it, my lady, he is holding something over you. What is he on about that he claims he will take to his grave? Eh? It must be something serious if he uses words like that."

Margaret said nothing. Lord Stanley tapped his fingers impatiently on the table.

"I sent Henry a great deal of money so that he can raise an army." She spoke quietly. She was not lying.

"My God, Margaret, you take risks! Richard is right. You have committed treason. You'll end up on the gallows, and I'll not be able to save you. I know Henry's cause means everything to you, but how far will you go to get what you want?"

Lord Stanley turned on his heels and walked furiously about the great room, hands behind his back.

"If you gave me your support, my Lord, I could succeed. Then we would be safe, and Henry would reward you well.

Lord Stanley stopped abruptly and turned to look at his wife.

"You'll never give up, will you?" She dropped her head and, biting her bottom lip, replied. "No, my Lord. While there is life in me, I will fight for my son's cause. I am determined he will be King of England.

Lord Stanley walked over to his wife and took her hands. "I'll see what I can do," he spoke so quietly she could hardly hear. "But first, we must deal with Collingbourne. The sooner he is out of the way, the better. His messenger is down in the kitchen now. He won't have the nerve to refuse to tell me of the man's whereabouts." Margaret smiled at him. At last, she had Stanley where she wanted him.

Chapter 20

Walter Hungerford carried a bottle of wine under his cloak as he walked through the prison door. He had come to visit his friend William Collingbourne. It had been weeks since Richard's men had dragged him from his hideout, tied his hands behind him, and lifted him onto a horse. Tumbling to the ground as they dragged him off the horse had caused him pain from the bruising for weeks.

Walter entered his cell, the guard locking the door behind him. Walter winced when he saw how pale and drawn Collingbourne looked. His clothes were creased and smelled of sweat and urine. Walter cursed Margaret under his breath. He pulled out the bottle of wine and placed it on the wooden bench. Then from each pocket in his cloak, he withdrew a goblet. Sunken eyes gratefully watched

Walter pour the wine into each goblet.

Walter's pockets were deep and nicely concealed within his cloak. He pulled out a small parcel wrapped in clean white linen. The eyes followed his every movement. Slowly he unwrapped the bundle and revealed two chunks of bread and several pieces of cheese. Collingbourne wrapped his tongue around the saliva that began to trickle in his mouth.

"You're a great friend, Walter, old boy." He couldn't wait to place the bread and cheese in his mouth.

"And how's that dog of mine? You giving him plenty of exercise?" Collingbourne missed his beautiful dog. He missed the walks, the fetching of the ball. "You'll have him if I don't get home, won't you, Walter? He knows you." Walter poured some more wine. "Of course, I will. You don't have to worry about Roary." He lifted his goblet and tapped William's. They both drank. Collingbourne drained the lot and wiped his lips. "That was a beautiful drop, Walter. I haven't tasted wine as good as that for a long time."

"You ought to enjoy it. It's one the best from my cellar. I hid it well beneath my cloak. Didn't want one of those fellows out there getting their eyes on it. They would confiscate it for sure." He paused then, with a pained expression, said, "They've issued the commission. I thought you would want to know. Richard is determined to make an example of you. Collingbourne took another long drink.

"The trouble is your case is considered extremely important." Walter continued to look troubled. Collingbourne smiled, took another drink, and smacked his lips, looking down at the empty goblet.

Walter tipped the rest of the bottle into it.

"You're a gentleman who has wielded great power. You've put them on the spot William. You were in power as late as July last year when the treason was committed. It looks bad, William."

Collingbourne continued to say nothing. Walter began to get impatient with him.

"Have you seen the list of those who have been commissioned for your trial?"

At last, William responded with a wry smile. "I hope I am important enough to rate a decent representation." Walter winced.

"You've got a decent representation, all right. There are to be two dukes and thirteen other lords, including Viscounts Lovell and Lisle; three barons, including Lord Stanley, together with the Lord Mayor of London and nine ordinary judges. How will that do you?" Walter's voice was tinged with bitterness. He hated to see his friend in this plight, and there was nothing he could do.

"Do you know the charge? He asked angrily. "It's bloody serious!" Collingbourne took another drink. Then he put down the goblet and put his hand on Walter's shoulder.

"It was stated that I offered a certain Thomas Yate eight pounds to go over to Brittany to the Earl of Richmond ……Damn it, Walter! I can't remember the wording, but I know I'm charged with trying to persuade Henry Tudor to come to England, where the people would rise in arms and levy war against Richard. Oh yes, and that I tried to persuade the French king to aid him."

"William, don't you realise the seriousness of it all? I know you're innocent, but if they can pin it on you, you'll not get off lightly. Tell them what you know – even if it involves Margaret. Save your skin, man, no one else is going to save you."

His voice began to break with the last words. Collingbourne sighed, finished his wine, and placed the goblet on the table.

"Walter, my old friend, I know it's serious, and I'll not get off lightly. I also know why I've been implicated. Now that's all I have to say. You've been a good friend…and…and."

A lump came into his throat. He tried to swallow but couldn't. Tears burned his eyes and then slowly poured down his face, sticky and wet. They gradually travelled along the lines in his face and dripped off the end of his nose and chin. Walter leant over to wipe the tears away from his friend's face and tasted the salt of his own as he licked his lips to prevent them from falling further.

"Did you give Margaret my letter?" Collingbourne spoke in a

husky voice.

Walter nodded. "And before you ask, I have arranged that she gets the money. It will be through me so none of the greedy swine's take it from her."

Collingbourne nodded. "You're a good friend Walter."

"She told me she is getting permission to visit you. Are you alright with that?"

Collingbourne looked concerned. "Do you think that is wise? I don't really want her to see me like this." He began to straighten his tunic.

"I don't think you will have a say in it, William. She is pretty upset about the whole thing. I didn't know she could be so fiery."

Collingbourne smiled. Yes, he had seen that mood on a few occasions. If she got something into her head, there was no stopping her. He sighed, looking about the room, his haggard face pale.

Walter patted him on the shoulder. "Of course, she wants to see you. She understands the seriousness of this trial, and I don't think how you look will stop her from what might be a last goodbye." He twisted a lip. "What about the Countess? Has she stooped to enter a prison to see the one she loves?" He was sorry he spoken the words as soon as they left his mouth. William screwed his lips and just stared ahead, not replying.

The trial took place at Guildhall early in December. The jury took their place, and Collingbourne was led in. Collingbourne agreed that he had written the verse but pleaded not guilty to charges of sedition and treason. Lord Stanley, still stinging from the message Collingbourne sent to his wife, scowled at him.

There had been much publicity and amusement about the rhyme. Lovell was extremely offended and pointed out that not only was the rhyme seditious, but it was downright insulting to refer to the King and his chief ministers as animals. Furthermore, it was insolent to suggest that King Richard was incapable of ruling his country; that he was unduly influenced by Catesby, Ratcliffe, and himself.

Collingbourne did not argue, but his smirk angered Lovell.

"Your insulting doggerel was a response from a man who was jealous because he had lost his offices in Wiltshire - an Office which Duchess Cecily, in her wisdom, chose to grant to me. Can you deny that?"

Lovell was pleased with his accusation that he believed showed Collingbourne in a poor light.

"Not at all," answered Collingbourne coolly. "Duchess Cecily made it quite clear she had no choice if her son chose to reward his….his…" He left the sentence unfinished.

"What are you implying?" stormed Lovell.

"My Lord," interrupted the Duke of Norfolk. "The accused has not denied his involvement in writing the verse. Harping on the topic is obscuring the more important charge of treason."

"I have not denied I wrote the verse," interrupted Collingbourne, "But I do deny they were acts of sedition."

"Just a little misplaced humour denigrating your sovereign and his ministers," sneered Lovell. Collingbourne ignored the remark.

"Isn't it true you enticed a Thomas Yates and gave him eight pounds to bear a message to the Earl of Richmond?" The Duke of Suffolk was now speaking.

"Certainly not." Collingbourne was indignant. "Why would I waste my money when there were others willing to take messages to the Earl of Richmond without payment?"

'And you sent messages to the French court that Richard would only trifle with their envoys since he meant to make war on France," continued the Duke of Suffolk.

"Absolute nonsense," replied Collingbourne angrily. "Louis XI neither sent nor, to my knowledge, *had* any intention of sending envoys to England."

"You are in contact with the French king, then?" The Duke spat out his question triumphantly.

"No, that's not true, but I can observe that French envoys never arrived." Collingbourne showed his irritation in his response.

"I have it from sound authority that you were involved in Buckingham's rebellion." Lord Stafford said. Collingbourne simply stared at him. He did not intend to answer questions that could implicate Margaret.'

"Well, he wasn't the only one involved there," said Norfolk acidly.

"Did you advise the Earl of Richmond to land in the south of England in the fall?" Lord Stafford spoke roughly.

"Did he land there?" Collingbourne answered.

"You know damn well he didn't!" Lovell blurted out. "But that wasn't thanks to you. It was the elements that prevented the landing - storms at sea!"

"That is hardly my doing. Perhaps the elements should be questioned!" Collingbourne said.

"You are surprisingly flippant, sir, for a man whose life hangs by a thread. Did you or did you not invite Henry Tudor to England?" Norfolk looked grave.

"I did not. I have been loyal to Edward and Richard all my life. These are trumped-up charges based on hearsay and rumours. King Richard has witnessed my services to the crown for many years.

"If you were innocent, why did you go into hiding?" Lovell fairly spat out the words.

Collingbourne replied in a husky voice. "I knew my life was in danger. Not for crimes I had supposedly committed, but for information I had acquired." There was a loud buzzing, and the Duke of Norfolk had to call for order several times before it was given.

Lord Stanley spluttered. He was worried. *Had Margaret kept something from him?*

"Such information that threatened your life must be very damming," Lord Stanley said silkily. "Will you enlighten us?"

He was taking a chance. Collingbourne had the opportunity to save himself. But Stanley knew he wouldn't take it and betray Margaret.

There was a strange silence while the court waited for his response. Collingbourne's face worked while he tried to keep control of his emotions. Finally, he answered with a simple "No."

"There you have it. He's lying! He's trying to bluff his way out of trouble." Lord Stanley spoke hurriedly, obviously anxious that the matter be settled once and for all. Margaret had had a very fortunate escape.

The commotion that broke out caused the Duke to go purple in the face as he tried to gain order.

There was no more discussion. Collingbourne was found guilty of high treason and condemned to be hanged, drawn, and quartered. The sentence was the extreme penalty for treason. The date of execution was 1st December 1484.

King Richard looked stoney faced when informed of the verdict. He had hoped for a different result. It wasn't consistent with Collingbourne's character at all. But then, he was under the spell of the Countess of Richmond. It should be her who paid the price, not him. His response was cold. It didn't reflect what was in his heart. "If he is guilty of the crime, he deserves the punishment."

On the proposed date in December Collingbourne was fastened to a wooden panel, and drawn by horses to Tower Hill where a new pair of gallows was erected for him. His wife, Margaret, clung to Walter's arm, trembling. Walter had begged her not to witness this terrible execution but she insisted. The sentence was carried out in the most barbaric way possible. Hardly conscious after being hanged, he was cut down, and thrown to the table. When the butcher put his hand into the bulk of his body, he moaned, "Oh Lord Jesus, yet more trouble." He screamed with pain as his bowels were ripped out of his belly, and thrown into the fire. Then he died.

Margaret collapsed at Walter's feet. He reached for her, but terrible pain made him groan and clutch his stomach as he witnessed his friend's entrails expand and burst with the heat of the fire. He began to retch. In all eternity, he would never forget the stench from the burning entrails. His eyes filled with tears. As others turned their heads, Walter watched as Collingbourne was beheaded. Then his body was chopped into quarters. The butcher, his face like stone, turned and walked away. Walter, as if in a trance, moved forward, bent and kissed his friend's familiar face, bloodied but at peace at last. He cursed Margaret, Countess of Richmond. It was she who deserved this punishment, not Collingbourne. Then he returned to William's widow and gathered her unconscious body into his arms. This was no place she should be.

Collingbourne was not the traitor he was perceived to be. True, he had briefly joined a meeting held to promote Buckingham. That was Margaret's doing. It was her way of implicating him; he had no idea it was a political meeting when he was taken to Buckingham's castle for a banquet.

In her scheming to get Collingbourne to change his allegiance to Henry Tudor, Margaret had deliberately deceived him by her lies that Stanley had told her Richard had murdered King Edward's sons. This, together with the knowledge that Richard had removed him from the position of steward to Duchess Cecily, a reward given by King Edward and given to Lovell, angered him. He vented his fury and disappointment with Richard by writing the verse and nailing it on the doors of St. Paul's cathedral.

It was Buckingham who alerted him to Margaret's ruthlessness. When she conceived the idea he had failed her, she had no more use for him. She deserted and betrayed him, ignoring his pleas for help. At first, Collingbourne did not believe it, but when he talked to Margaret, he knew Buckingham had told the truth. He could never trust her again. She weaved lies with the truth to suit her ambition. She used people like pawns in the game she played. When they were needed no more, she destroyed them. Colliingbourne had been duped by the woman he loved. A gentleman to the last, he had not betrayed her.

Chapter 21

Richard sat in his favourite chair in front of a blazing fire. It was early December, and the first fall of snow had already transformed the garden into slender shadows and sculptured shapes. Relaxed and comfortable, he watched flakes of snow twirling and dancing. Soon the heavy tapestried curtains would be drawn to keep in the warmth. Darkness fell very early this time of year. His thoughts turned to the news he had received earlier in the day. Lord Stanley had spoken almost triumphantly. Collingbourne had been found guilty. He was to receive the harshest punishment. Richard was aware that Collingbourne had been intimately associated with Stanley's wife, the Countess of Richmond, for many years. He wondered just how much influence she had on Collingbourne, she couldn't be trusted, and he suspected she was behind the rumours about Collingbourne's disloyalty. Stanley's gloating troubled him. He wished he had pardoned Collingbourne. He had the power to do so. He had wondered what Edward would have done, but he knew Collingbourne would never have betrayed Edward. He had deliberately distanced himself from the decision and replied. "If the man is guilty, he deserves the punishment." No one could say he had been unjust; there were 25 who judged him. Yet, there was this niggling suspicion that it hadn't been a fair trial.

He pushed the matter from his mind and thought about his two nephews. It had taken quite some time to convince young Edward that it was not Richard's fault that he was no longer king. For weeks his nephew had refused to speak. He had warned his brother, Richard, to do the same. Although they had been removed gently from the Tower persuaded rather than ordered, and he had personally supervised the journey of both boys to Middleham Castle, where they were safe, young Edward clearly resented it. He believed he was king, although he had been told that his uncle Gloucester had been crowned instead of him. He was confused and had demanded to see his mother. His demands were ignored. Richard understood Edward had been taught it shouldn't be like that. The king must always be obeyed. But no one obeyed him. He had tried tantrums, but that hadn't worked either. The guard had simply walked away. The boy would have observed that everyone trembled when his father was displeased. Richard recalled how unknown to young Edward, he had heard him calling for his Uncle Woodville. "Tell me, dear uncle, what am I doing wrong? Why didn't you tell me how difficult it is to be king? Please come back to me. My Uncle Gloucester says my life is in danger. I am so very scared." Richard had turned away, saddened that his nephew did not trust him as he did his Woodville uncle. But it was hardly surprising when since he was three years old, young Prince Edward had his own household at Ludlow Castle and Earl Rivers; his Uncle Anthony Woodville was responsible for his upbringing and education.

Richard had decided there had to be a way to get him to understand that he had not usurped his throne. Edward was an educated young man, and Richard had shown him copies of the Act. He had explained that, according to Bishop Stillingham, his father was already married when he married his mother, and as a consequence, he and his siblings were illegitimate. It had taken time, but gradually young Edward had accepted the facts and realised that his Uncle Gloucester was doing his best to keep him safe. They had discussed what could be done. It was Edward's suggestion that he and his brother be allowed to live in a place far from London.

Richard had agreed it could be done. They would need a different name and live far apart. That saddened Edward. He felt responsible for his younger brother, but he acknowledged they would be safer apart.

"Who knows what the future holds," Richard had spoken kindly. "Maybe when you are older, and people have forgotten, you will be able to be together again. I do not intend to pretend that your lives will be easy. There will always be fear that you will be a threat to who is on the throne. I do not envy you. Nor will you know the whereabouts of the other. It is too dangerous. What you don't know cannot be forced out of you. Torture can break the strongest of men to reveal what they should not." He had felt such pity that they had to endure so much, so young.

He had sent the younger boy, Richard, to Burgundy. Weeks ago, he had messaged his sister, Duchess Margaret, by a man he would trust his life with. His message was in code that he knew his sister could break. Would she care for their young nephew with her life? Give him a new name and life. If the answer was yes, he would arrange it immediately. Margaret had followed the scandal of the disappearance of the princes from the Tower. News travelled fast. She hadn't believed the rumours that Richard had murdered them and was extremely angry at the suggestion. She wasn't surprised she had this request. Richard was her brother who could be confident she would help if she could.

Queen Anne suggested they disguise the young prince before he left. His head shaved and covered by a blonde wig was enough.

He travelled with the same trusted man who had taken the name, Sir John Clifford. Young Richard was to be known as his son. Duchess Margaret made plans before their arrival. Richard knew no more; only the property was in rural Burgundy with an annual income to keep them in great comfort for the rest of their lives. He chose not to ask more.

Sir Thomas Markenfield held in his hand a letter from King Richard who was on his way to visit. He had urgent business he wished to discuss with Thomas and his brother Robert. Richard had been a good friend to both the brothers and very generous in the past. It would be pleasant to see him at Markenfield Hall, although it was disappointing Queen Anne and their son Edward were not well enough to travel. Sir Thomas was even more surprised when Richard arrived on his own.

Greetings over, and refreshments enjoyed; Richard settled in a comfortable chair in the great room. He was pleased to see the roaring fire; the weather had been cold, and his feet throbbed and tingled. Both Robert and Thomas were now seated.

"This must seem an extraordinary visit Sir Thomas, but I am sure you recognise the importance and confidentiality necessary by my lack of men. Indeed, the few I brought with me settled in a nearby town. Thomas was a tall man with broad shoulders. His dark hair hung, almost touching his shoulders. Fearsome on the battlefield, Thomas had been ready to support Richard during

Buckingham's rebellion. He was the same age as Richard, and they had been friends nearly all their lives. Robert was younger but an equally strapping man and as loyal to Richard as his brother.

"I must admit I am curious about this visit," Thomas's voice boomed. Robert nodded in agreement. Richard leaned forward. "The point is, what I am about to ask of you might seem strange, for I desire Robert to journey to a remote village in Devon very discreetly. I have granted him the Manor of Coldridge in Devon. There are some rather complicated arrangements with this grant. There is also a Stewardship of the Royal Deer Park." He stopped and looked from man to man. They looked interested but confused. Neither spoke but waited for the king to continue. Richard smiled. "Robert, it may appear strange that I am sending you to the end of the earth while your brother here has enjoyed gifts close by. The truth is simple. I do not wish to draw attention to this matter. Few will be interested in where you have gone or why, but if I sent Thomas, eyes would follow, knowing he works by my side."

Thomas stood and offered to fill Richard's jug with ale. "The mystery thickens! Do get to the point, Richard."

"Once Robert has introduced himself in Devon, and is recognised as the Lord of the Manor and also Steward of the Deer Park, I want you Robert, to appoint the necessary staff needed. Existing staff if you wish. Then to engage a boy, we will call John Evans, who, when he is old enough, will own the property for life.

He paused, waiting for a reaction. Thomas looked sharply at Richard, who was fingering his ring. His face broke into a grin. Then he spoke. "Would this boy be about twelve or thirteen years old?" Richard smiled, there was amusement in his eyes. He knew he couldn't fool Thomas. "Yes. He is to be guided and shown how to manage the estate. He has had some training of running a household. Thomas chortled. "You're a dark horse, your majesty."

Richard smiled. You will be well rewarded, Robert.

"When do I go?" Robert was keen. Richard withdrew a roll of parchment from his robe. These are the documents you need. Everything is provided and ready for you. He leaned and passed the documents to Robert. A grumbling of Richard's stomach caused laughter. "Your majesty, it seems you are ready for a good meal. The kitchens have been busy, and I see my man is indicating that it is time to eat." Sir Thomas could hardly conceal laughter, but Richard thanked him heartily. He was indeed, very hungry.

While in Yorkshire, Richard took the opportunity to call on his nephew Edward at Middleham Castle. The boy was kicking a ball up against a wall in a private garden. Richard remembered doing the same. Edward looked up when he heard his uncle approach. He caught the ball as it rebounded from the wall and threw it at his uncle. Richard neatly caught it and tossed it back. He sat on the edge of a low garden wall.

"It's been arranged. Would you like to know where you will

go? Edward walked over and sat next to him.

"You are to travel to a remote village In Devon under the name of John Evans. There is a manor there that is gifted to you and is your home. Not quite as grand as your household in Wales, but you will be unknown and safe. You have been given the Parkership of this property, but until you have learned how to manage it yourself, you will be shown by a very able and loyal man, Robert Brackenfield. When you feel confident you can manage the household and the estate yourself, you will be the Lord of the Manor and free to live in peace. Brackenfield will return to Yorkshire or will be granted an estate of his own nearby. Edward sat quietly, thinking. He couldn't deny he was scared. He bit his lip and looked at his uncle.

"You will not be on your own, Edward. You will make friends. One day you will marry and have children. Life can be good. But remember, Edward, you are no longer royalty in the eyes of the people, so your wardrobe will no longer be trimmed with ermine. It is very important that you behave like a member of the nobility but not as a king. However, the excellent training and education given by your Woodville uncle will not go to waste."

Edward stood silent for a while. Richard watched as his nephew tried to take in all he had said. He knew fate had lifted the heavy robe of responsibility from his nephew but wondered if Edward appreciated it.

"Will I see my mother again?" The simple question touched Richard. How much sadness this boy had seen in his short life, the loss of so many he loved. He put a hand on the boy's shoulder and looked him in the eye. "I believe you will. She knows where you will be. If it is in her power, she will visit you and quite soon." Richard noted the boy's bottom lip tremble. "Come, Edward. I need to go back to London. Let us spend a pleasant evening together. You can see the gifts your aunt has sent to you for Christmas."

Richard had chosen his favourite stallion to make his journey back to London. He rode with three or four men but felt no need for companionship. He had received news from Anne that their son was too ill to take to London for the Christmas celebrations. They would need to leave him. Occasions like this made him wish Edward was alive. He fondly remembered the early days of his marriage when they had more time as a family. Duty! Always duty! How he longed for peaceful days. True, there were times when rebellions broke out, and he needed to quell them, but life was much easier without the crown. Yet there were those who looked greedily to take it. Henry Tudor, for one. He had already tried once, and perhaps it had been good fortune that England was battered by storms that prevented his landing. But what of next time? Why in God's name would Collingbourne have invited Henry Tudor to come to England to take the crown? Was he really that enraged that he had asked his mother, Duchess Cecily, to give Lovell the position Collingbourne had? He had hoped Collingbourne would have challenged him about it. He wasn't slow to say what he thought in the past. He quite expected some sort of confrontation from the man. He could never quite work out whether Collingbourne had been involved in Buckingham's rebellion. He thought a slight punishment would act as a warning. If Collingbourne was innocent, why wasn't he man enough to ask why? Yet he knew Collingbourne did not lack courage. It troubled Richard, the nagging guilt, that by not supporting Collingbourne, he had let Edward down.

But it was Buckingham's betrayal that had grieved him so much. Who would have thought that a man could turn so suddenly? A man who had offered him the crown and pushed him to take it yet within months wanted it himself. Richard had heard rumours that Buckingham thought he, and not Henry Tudor, was entitled to the throne of England. It was all the work of the Bishop of Ely, and that led back to Margaret, who had blatantly committed treason against him. But what could he do? He had taken her properties and wealth but given it to her husband, warning to keep her in control. He would have liked to have sent her to the gallows, but there was Stanley. Damn the man. Whose side was he really on? He needed to keep him close. Stanley and his son were far too powerful.

Christmas was usually a joyful time, but the Christmas of 1484 Richard and Anne were without their precious son. His sudden death last spring at their castle in Nottingham, had devastated the couple. Richard prayed to God asking if he was being punished for his part in the death of his brother George. Or had God taken his son because he had taken the crown from his brother's son young Edward? Was the death of his son his fault? Queen Anne despaired, not only had she lost her beloved son, but she could have no more children. Both king and queen were almost mad with grief. From the death of his son, Richard always referred to their castle in Nottingham, Castle of his Care.

However, grief was a luxury in which Richard could not indulge. Matters of state could not be ignored. Elizabeth had kept her word and allowed the princesses to attend court. Richard was pleased to see them extravagantly dressed and happy. Anne was delighted with the beautiful jewels he had presented her in the privacy of their rooms. The richness of the rubies in a necklace contrasted with her pale face. He said nothing, but he was gripped with fear. She was his most precious jewel, but she was fading before his eyes. When he held her close to him to take the floor, she felt as fragile as a bird, and soon weakness overcame her. He led her to a chair. She watched him whirling around the room with his niece Elizabeth. So young, beautiful, and full of energy. Anne tried not to envy her. She knew her time was near. How cruel that she must go.

Later, when they were alone together in their bedchamber, she kissed his cheek and sat close. He took her hand and pressed it to his lips. 'What is it, my dearest? Do you feel a little better now we are away from the noise?"

"Richard, you know as I do that my time is almost come." He kissed her lips, hushing her from uttering the words he dreaded to hear.

She leaned her head against his chest as he stroked her head. So thin and frail. He hated to see her like this.

"When I saw you dancing with Elizabeth, I was jealous. How I wish I had the beauty and energy that she has. But I realise you will need a young wife to be your queen and who will give you an heir." He felt a lump in his throat. It was difficult to swallow. "Don't speak that way, my darling." His voice sounded a croak.

"I wish I could stay by your side forever, but I know that cannot be. Please, Richard, do not waste time. Look for a suitable bride who you can love and who will share the burden you have. It is my wish that I can leave this world knowing you will not grieve. We have spent far too much time grieving for our son. Soon I will be with him, and you, my darling, must know we will be there in spirit by your side, just as I know Edward is always with us."

Richard could listen no more. He pulled Anne close to him and buried his head in her chest, even then noticing how the flesh was melting away. He lost his kingliness and dignity; he was afraid and could no longer hold back his tears. "Anne, don't leave me. I cannot do this on my own. I don't want another queen. She could never replace you." Anne felt smothered from his tight clasp and gently pushed him away a little.

"My darling, she will not replace me; there is room for us both. It will make me so happy to know she will be there by your side when I cannot."

By February, Anne was confined to her bed. Her physicians warned Richard that her illness was contagious. He must not share her chamber. His world became dark. By March, it was clear that she was dying. Despite the physicians warning, he insisted on sitting by her bedside for hours. He read to her, prayed, and talked about nothing, really. Although she smiled when she saw him, she soon drifted to sleep. His depression deepened. Why was God punishing him? Was he wrong to accept the crown? Why had his only son been taken from him? He had shown kindness to Edward's boys and sent them to safety when their lives were threatened. He had taken care of his brother George's children when their father was executed for treason. He had begged Edward to give George another chance, but Edward was adamant.

Anne gave a little groan. Perspiration dampened her hair. She tossed and turned. He spoke to her gently as he dipped a flannel in the bowl of scented water placed beside her bed and gently wiped her brow. Why was God taking her too?

Was it an omen that on the day she died, there was a great eclipse of the sun? There were those who thought it was. Richard watched in despair as her body was born to Westminster Abbey. He buried her near the south door that led into St. Edward's chapel.

Richard knew people were whispering he had poisoned his wife. It pained him to hear it, but the pain of kissing his wife for the last time was so much worse. He knew the truth. If God had answered his prayers, He would have allowed Anne to live. Life was cruel. He had lost all those he loved. But the living must continue their journey. Wearily he walked to join Ratcliffe and Catesby, who had asked for an audience.

Ratcliffe and Catesby sat nervously awaiting the King. A formidable task lay before them. It had been rumoured the King intended to marry Princess Elizabeth. Richard swept into the room. He also had heard the rumour. It was true; he had enjoyed dancing with the young princess, so why not? It had been Christmas, a time to be jolly. He found her company entertaining. He had not left Anne to do so. First, the rumour he had poisoned his wife, and now this nonsense.

Catesby bowed as Richard entered. He sensed the King was agitated and gave a sidelong glance at Ratcliffe. Richard was easily upset these days and often displayed impatience. The King seated himself. An uncomfortable silence pursued. It was customary to wait for the King to start a conversation. Irritated, Richard began. "You wish to confer with me on an important matter?" His voice was cold. He knew what it was about, but he was not going to make it easy for them. Ratcliffe began.

"Your majesty, about this matter of you wishing to marry Princess Elizabeth." He gave what he hoped was a humorous laugh. "Of course, we know it is ridiculous to even entertain such a match…"

Richard raised an eyebrow. "You do not think Princess Elizabeth, Edward's daughter, is good enough?" Catesby intervened. "The young lady in question is Elizabeth Woodville, illegitimate daughter of late King Edward."

"You think I am not aware of that!" Richard's response was clipped.

"Good God, Richard…" a glare from the king stopped Catesby in his track. Richard stood and began pacing the room.

"Do you two gentlemen, my supposed friends, think I am foolish to marry my illegitimate niece?

"We only wished to advise that your friends in the North would no longer support you if you do not publicly deny it. They simply won't tolerate it!"

Richard stopped pacing and stared at both men coldly. "Could it be you fear for your lives because Elizabeth may wish to avenge the death of Rivers and Lord Richard Grey?" The air was electric. Catesby shot a quick look at Ratcliffe before he spoke. Was it just himself who could feel the tension? He continued anyway.

"Your majesty, such a marriage would be abhorred by many; even the Pope could not condone such a degree of consanguinity. We are your friends. Our only wish is to protect you." To their surprise, Richard, with an instant change of mood, laughed.

"My Lords, the enjoyment of such a rumour is that it makes Henry Tudor very uncomfortable. He seeks to take her for his bride and unite Lancastrians and Yorkists. He knows the Princess is the lynchpin to his success in taking the throne. I don't intend to cause another rebellion by marrying Elizabeth," he laughed cynically, "but I believe Elizabeth rather fancies the idea herself. No, I will remove her to Sheriff Hutton Castle, safely out of his reach. She can enjoy the company of the Earl of Warwick." He turned to leave the room, then stopped. "Don't you realise such rumours are being circulated by seditious persons who wish to promote discord between us, my lords?" He rubbed his hands together, then nodded as if making a decision. "Yes, we will make a public announcement denying this rumour and assure my people it is not going to happen." He laughed again heartily this time. "Oh, but I did enjoy thinking about Henry Tudor and his mother's panic when they thought I was about to thwart their plans."

Catesby looked thoughtful, then spoke. "If marriage to Princess Elizabeth is Tudor's lynchpin to success, why not marry her off to someone else?" Richard smiled. "It's a matter of honour. I must live by my conscience. I will not marry Elizabeth "off", as you describe it, until this matter of the crown is settled once and for all. It may be her wish to marry the man if Margaret, Countess of Richmond has her way and is successful in her ambition.

Chapter 22

Richard lived for months under the dark cloud that had descended over him when Anne died. He was alone and preferred to stay that way. Fortunately, since the end of Buckingham's rebellion, there had been peace. He knew that peace would end once Henry Tudor had managed to beg enough money to attack. Richard was kept informed of Tudor's progress by his agents. It was not until the middle of June that he arrived home at the Castle of his Care.

Sitting in his beautiful gardens, he felt no peace. His thoughts turned to Henry Tudor. He felt a growing anger against him as he learned from his agents that Tudor partisans were spreading propaganda that attacked his honour and disturbed the peace in England. Margaret, Stanley's wife, was one of the greatest instigators—she and her servant Reynold Bray who was as cunning as a fox. John Morton, another whom he had heard, was one of the leaders of the campaign and Thomas Rotherham. He knew the traitors who had gone to support Tudor. Grey, Marquess of Dorset, was another, but he had attempted to return to England when Elizabeth had written to say Richard had pardoned him, but he was caught. Henry didn't really trust him but considered it safer for Dorset to be under his watch. Richard's informer made the point that Henry had decided he couldn't wait longer to attack after Dorset had attempted to steal away. Now it was just a waiting game.

Richard was not surprised when Lord Stanley asked the question he had been waiting for. It was late afternoon. Stanley commented on the fact he had served Edward for a decade, and now Richard, without a break. His position as Steward of Richard's Royal Household required him to be in close attendance upon the King. Richard's face was expressionless. He let Stanley continue. "It is years since I had a break, apart from a week here and there. Rest will help me prepare for the invasion, and of course, if it does occur, I will be well positioned to rally my men for our cause." Richard said nothing. He listened attentively. It appeared to be a reasonable request, but he knew as well as Stanley that it wasn't. He marveled at the way Thomas so smoothly planned his move. They both knew there was a reason why

Richard kept Stanley by his side and why Stanley did not seek to leave the court. Stanley and his brother were experts at developing an attitude of ambiguity. It was never clear which side they would support, but they always ended up on the winning side. It was incredible that they frequently escaped the consequence of betrayal, and as a result, the Stanleys commanded one of the greatest seignorial systems in England.

Richard was no fool. He was well aware of Stanley's power. He also understood why Margaret, Countess of Richmond, had married him. The Stanleys always tailored their allegiance to their advantage, and Margaret would make sure her husband understood the advantage was to support Henry. Richard began fingering his ring as he studied Stanley's face. He had always known that Thomas would request permission to depart when the time was right. Clearly, the invasion was close. Richard was cognizant of the uncertainty the House of Stanley would support him. He could end the matter now by simply holding Stanley in custody until the invasion was over. Reason told him it was the rational thing to do, but although he didn't understand why, a deeper compulsion than rationality moved him. He wanted allegiance given freely, not by force. Stanley must be free to ride away if he chooses to do so. Surely, loyalty is given out of respect and love, not fear. Of course, there are always those who feign loyalty for what they can get or what they might lose. But that was not the kind of loyalty he desired. Stanley coughed. He wanted an answer. Richard smiled. He promised Stanley he would give the matter consideration and let him know within a few days.

Catesby stared in disbelief when Richard gave them the news that Stanley wanted to retire for a while. His three councillors had gathered with him to discuss this latest news. Ratcliffe snorted. "It sounds to me that he knows something we don't. Of course, you told him to wake up to himself. He knows damn well Tudor is about to invade."

Richard began to wring his hands. "Yes, he knows, but he argues that he will be better placed to rally his men to the King's cause."

"The King's cause. Poppycock!" Catesby exploded. "More like rally his men for his own cause. Richard, you know you can't trust him. Isn't that why you keep him close?" He guffawed.

"Exactly. But we both know it is a strategy. Kendall looked grave. "You are not considering letting him go, are you? It would be madness to do so with the landing of Tudor so imminent." Both Catesby and Ratcliffe nodded, watching Richard intently. Richard fingered his ring.

How could he explain he wanted his subjects to give their allegiance willingly? It wasn't justice to lock Stanley up before he committed a crime. 'Innocent until proven guilty'. That is what he had espoused to his people, particularly to his judges and legal officers. He wanted his people to be just to each other. He must lead by example. Was he considering letting Stanley go? Yes. To do otherwise would reveal to Stanley that he didn't trust him. His councillors tried to persuade him to rethink what he was about to do. He understood their concern and agreed to insist that Stanley send Lord Strange to act as his deputy.

It was all very polite. Richard brought up the subject as the two men were taking a breath of fresh air after an extremely busy day.

"I have looked favourably on your request for leave, Thomas." Stanley stopped walking, surprised it was so easy. "But," Richard continued, "I am sure you understand I must have a deputy during your absence. I see no reason to refuse your leave if you send Lord Strange to act on your behalf." Stanley was not fooled; he knew Richard was taking his son as hostage, and Richard was aware he knew it. The polite charade continued, and Stanley willingly acquiesced. He was happy. The door was open for him to return if he wished, but he had his escape route if he made another choice. What about his son? Well, he had others, but would Richard really harm him? Did it fit with his idea of justice? No, he was certain his son was safe.

That night Richard dreamed. He was sitting in an enormous chair made of nothing but air. It was peaceful, and he felt content. Before him stood a man, he didn't recognise him at all, yet he was sure he knew him. A kindness flowed from him that made Richard unconcerned.

The man was speaking, yet there was no voice; somehow, the voice was in his head. "You have been tested. How do you think you have fared so far? Richard was surprised. "Tested? I do not understand."

"Umm. What kind of king are you? Are you the man you wish to be?" Richard thought about the question.

"Am I?" It was a question, not an answer.

"You were given the task of having your nephew crowned. Instead, you took the crown for yourself. What say you to that?"

"It was not my decision. He was illegitimate, and once I knew that, I had no choice but to ask the people." It was they who made the decision, and they who begged me to take the crown." The man smiled.

"You sent your brother's sons away? Was that kind? Two young boys sent out in the world on their own."

Richard was indignant. "I hope they will have a happier life than shut in the Tower. I heard there were moves to rescue them. They were in danger from she who wants my crown for her son." The man smiled again but made no judgement."

"And Collingbourne. He was loyal to your family and worked hard for Edward, your brother. Yet, you did not hear him when he needed you. Was justice done to him?"

Richard covered his eyes. "I know. I know. We all make mistakes."

"Do you want Henry Tudor to land in England so you can kill him?" The man looked serious.

"I am angered by him. He is dishonouring me and causing friction in my kingdom. He wants to take my throne. I must defend my kingdom."

The man moved closer. "You could prevent his coming if you find a husband for Elizabeth. You can save yourself if you get rid of Stanley. He will betray you; you know that."

Richard clenched his fists. Frustrated, he raised his voice. "Yes, I know. But that is not the King I want to be." The man smiled and then disappeared. Richard awoke. What did the dream mean?

The dream played repeatedly in Richard's brain the following day, particularly his outcry, "That is not the King I want to be."

He thought about Collingbourne. He wished he had talked to him. Perhaps the man was not guilty as charged. He thought of the way Tudor had dishonoured him. So many lies. If Collingbourne had betrayed him, had Margaret poisoned his mind? What if Collingbourne believed his anger was justified? If Margaret had lied just as Henry lied about him and Collingbourne had found out she had betrayed him, would he be justified in betraying her?

Maybe Collingbourne's actions were the result of falsehoods, and he, like himself, had been deceived? He had heard rumours about that fact.

If taking the blame himself rather than betraying her, had Collingbourne shown absolute loyalty to Margaret? Loyalty given with love. Isn't that what he believed in? But no, you cannot give loyalty without trust. One must always be true to oneself first.

He had allowed Collingbourne to be put to death in the most barbaric way. That was not the king he wanted to be.

Dreams were messages. He hadn't understood this message. If only Anne was with him. She always understood things. Thinking of Anne made him realise how lonely he was—big castles, with only him to wander around them. Perhaps Catesby was right. He should consider the Portugal bride he had been urged to take.

Within days Stanley had gone. Richard felt some sadness as he watched him leave Castle of his Care. He stood there watching the lone figure get smaller as it travelled forward, finally just a dot, then nothing but a cloud of dust. For some reason, he never did understand why, he went to Stanley's chamber. Was it the fear that this was the first step of betrayal? Did he need to confirm it was true? The large room with its heavy damask curtains, boasting rich colours, had not been attended to by the servants. As he moved around the room, his senses recognised the musky aroma of sandalwood that usually accompanied Stanley. Not strong, just a suggestion drifting gently through the air.

He glanced at the window aimlessly. Then he saw it. A roll of parchment caught behind the curtain on the floor. His first instinct was to leave it, but his curiosity got the better of him, and he picked it up. The seal was broken. But he recognised it at once.

Fascinated, he unrolled the document. Slowly he read the letter not meant for his eyes. It was to Margaret, Countess of Richmond, from William Collingbourne. He was stunned. His eyes returned to a paragraph that appeared to jump from the page.

However, although I cannot condone what you have done, it is not for me to pass judgement. God will do that. I can only give you my word, dearest, that I will not betray you. Your secret will go with me to my grave. Tears come to my manly eyes when I think that after all our years of love together, you didn't have enough trust in me to know that your secret would be safe, however much I deplored your actions. Margaret, the disappointment and your lack of trust in me have broken my heart. There is nothing Richard can do that could cause the pain you have inflicted on me. I know the words that have reached Richard have come from your own sweet lips, and you knew they were lies and exactly what the consequence of such words meant.

It is our downfall that we men underestimate the power and wit of women. What fools we are. Nevertheless, I remember you in my prayers and forgive you.

Richard felt weakness in his legs. He sat on the bed and, hands shaking, read the letter again. How did this letter get here? Stanley must have seen it and taken it from his wife. Why? Stanley had allowed the verdict to be guilty when Collingbourne was clearly protecting Margaret, and the truth had not been heard. He wondered what the secret was that Collingbourne took to his grave. Once this battle was over, he would do with Margaret what he should have done in the first place. He would get the truth from her about Collingbourne. He could feel his anger rising. He left the room without a further glance. Did Stanley leave the letter in the room for him to see? But why hide it behind the curtain? Why not simply give it to him? No. He couldn't do that; it implicated his wife. Richard's mind raced. He strode out of the building. What should he do? He wondered if Stanley would realise he had left such an important document behind. It was not the time to deal with this matter now. Tudor had set sail. He had sent to his chancellor for the Great Seal. All he could do was wait now.

High on the rocks, alone with his thoughts, he walked. He had no army with him, only the knights and esquires of his Body and certain of his most close followers and their servants. He had told no one about the letter, but he thought about it constantly. He made up his mind. Collingbourne must be pardoned. His manor, and all that had been taken, must be returned.

Once this battle was over, it would be done. But if he should lose? Who would pardon Collingbourne, then?

On August 11^{th,} a messenger arrived with the news that Henry Tudor had landed in Milford Haven, South Wales, on Sunday, August 7th. Now was the time for action. The long wait was over.

Chapter 23

The night of the battle had advanced. Richard and his commanders decided the royal army would occupy Ambien Hill early in the morning. Richard bid his captains good night but was not ready to rest himself. In the darkness, he could see Lord Stanley's fires in the distance. Richard knew in his heart that whoever was victorious in the morrow, England would never be the same. He didn't doubt that Henry would rule like a despot walking in Louis XI's footsteps. But what of himself if he was the victor? Richard recognised his obsession for justice had not served him well. He had tried to make a fairer and happier England, particularly for the ordinary people without land and title. He had wanted oppression gone and justice for all, whatever class of society. In that, he had failed. Had he trusted too much? Was it weak to trust?

It had been Edward's near destruction pardoning George so many times. He had been critical of his older brother for taking George's life, but how long can one hold the crown by showing mercy to those who betray you? He thought he had known men. How shattering it had been when he learned of Buckingham's betrayal. How unprepared he was. Already on this battlefield, he had evidence of betrayal of Northumberland, who requested to hold a position in the rear. He had tersely agreed, it was little use arguing, but he knew Northumberland was not totally committed despite the fact that those who followed him had no idea of his treachery. He sighed. No more would he tolerate betrayal. If he should ride victorious from this battle, he would be more ruthless in demanding obedience.

He slept little. At first, his dreams were bittersweet. Anne came to him, her arms outstretched to clasp him, but she dissolved into the air when he reached her. His son Edward laughed and ran before him, calling over his shoulder for his father to follow. He ran like the wind after his little boy, but he was always out of reach. Drenched in perspiration, he tossed and turned—then Edward, his brother, young and strong, charged on his horse beside him. "Well done!" he called, waving his sword up high. Richard glowed with pleasure. They had defeated the Lancastrians together.

He awoke suddenly. It was a dream. How grand it had felt to

see Edward. If only he were riding beside him today. The dark cloud suddenly dropped over him like a cloak. He had never felt such despair. Suddenly it all seemed so pointless. If Tudor was victorious, he would rule with an iron hand, crushing the House of York and ruling by fear. Men were fools. Was that the kind of King they wanted? He knew there was one thing he must do. In the early light of dawn, he took his quill and wrote a letter. He carefully folded the letter, and pressed his seal firmly, and addressed it to Margaret, Countess of Richmond. Walking out in the clear morning, he sought the young squire he knew he could trust, not much older than his nephew Edward, who was now safely settled miles away.

He whispered in the squire's ear. "Do you know Margaret, Countess of Richmond?" The boy nodded. "I do that, your majesty." Richard patted his head. "Good. If you should hear I am slain, go. Ride as hard as you can until you find her. Give this message in her hands only. If I am victorious, wait until you can place it in my own. Do you understand? Do you swear to do this?" The boy breathed a sigh of pleasure, proud that the King had given him this clearly important task. "Mind you, tell no one." Richard slipped a gold coin into his hand. The boy crossed his heart. "You can trust me, your majesty, and mum's the word." Richard laughed.

The sound of the stirring camp met his ears. Horses neighing to each other, restless stamping, keen to be on the move. The chief men gathered outside Richard's tent were surprised to see the king approach them. They looked concerned. He guessed he looked pale. The sleepless night had taken its toll. Officers were encouraging their men to breakfast. Richard ate a little. He was keen to start. Soon they were moving down Harper's Hill. The morning was fresh, and riding in the cool air felt good. Stanley's troops had made no move. Richard sent a message commanding him to come at once if he valued his son's life. He was not surprised when Stanley sent a message it did not suit him to go to the King. As for his son, he had others.

Richard cursed. He knew Stanley was testing him. Furious, he ordered a squire to see to Lord Strange's execution at once but immediately withdrew the order. He wasn't ready to become the tyrant he needed to be. He changed the order. Stanley's son was to be kept under strict guard.

As the groups found their places, Richard scanned the battlefield. Where was Tudor? He called for his men who had keen sight and skill in heraldic bearings. He sent several with instructions to find out the whereabouts of Henry Tudor.

Not long before, one of his men with keen sight spotted Henry and came running to inform his King; Richard received the news with pleasure. The dark cloak fell from his shoulders. He felt a strange peace not experienced for many years. Here was the opportunity of which he had dreamed. Its success or failure was not in his mind. There was no room for decision. It had been made. A surprise attack – a quick glorious victory. He smiled. Edward was standing by his side, urging him on. He did not question his presence. They both knew the outcome could be an absolute disaster, but victory would be brilliant.

He could visualize hurling himself at the man who had spread untruthful rumors to dishonor him, destroying his peace of mind and causing unrest in his kingdom. Whatever the outcome, it would end this nightmare, end his agony of spirit and slaughter of his subjects.

His sense of justice would not allow others to risk their life for a fight that was between Henry and himself. He was the defender of England and, beside him, the sworn defenders of his body. He would include no one else on this perilous journey. Better for everyone; it be quick and done with whatever the outcome.

Catesby tried to persuade Richard to take flight. Now was the time. It was too risky to continue. Richard determinedly shook his head. Watching Catesby walk away, Richard, assisted by his squire, mounted his white horse. The Household followed suit. Turning his horse toward them, Richard's heart warmed. These were his household, Knights, and Esquires, who were truly loyal. His eyes slowly searched each face. Sir Richard Ratcliffe, Sir James Harrington, Sir Marmaduke Constable, Sir Thomas Burgh,

Sir Ralph Assheton, Sir Thomas Pilkington, John Sapcote. Humphrey and Thomas Stafford. Then close behind him, Constable of the Tower, Sir Robert Brackenbury, and even his secretary, John Kendall. He, too, was in full armor, ready to fight by Richard's side. His true friends, Francis Viscount Lovell, and Sir Robert Percy, were also there.

How proud he felt. These were men who really knew him. Richard rose in his stirrups and called loudly to all. "We ride to seek Henry Tudor." Before he closed his visor, he saw once again his brother Edward on his white stallion, in full armor, ready to go with him.

Richard, riding forth with his crown glittering in the sunshine, spared no effort to reach his target. Some of his Household had tried to dissuade him from wearing it on his helmet. Too easily seen; it labeled him. Richard responded that he would live, and die, King of England. He charged ahead; his target was closer.

Henry Tudor experienced the fright of his life as he observed the King getting closer, swinging his axe against William Brandon's sword. Was the man insane? Tudor jerked his horse in all directions. Should he flee? But no, his army would lose faith. Tudor watched as Richard's men tried to surround and protect him. One pulled at his bridle. Richard was almost upon him. Tudor's lips went dry. He was terrified. He felt tingling creep up the back of his neck under his armor. His heart pounded. A squire shouted and pointed. Richard turned, and his men thrust their horses before him. They had made an escape route. Too late, he saw Sir William Stanley's cavalry approaching at speed. A squire offered Richard a fresh horse. As soon as he was seated, instead of taking the escape, he turned and spurred towards Henry Tudor.

It ended quickly, just as Richard had hoped. Despite his shouts of "Treason", his household could protect him no more. Dozens of weapons smashed him pitilessly. He was surrounded by his foes who beat him until life left him, and he fell to the ground.

As the last breath left him, Edward swooped and lifted him to his horse. Richard looked down and saw his body roughly stripped and thrown over a horse. Edward spoke. "One day, the world will learn the truth."

Margaret, Countess of Richmond, was delighted when she received the news her son was victorious. The Stanleys had saved the day. Her life dream had become a reality. She spared no thoughts for those who had lost.

After Henry had arrived in London and set up his court, Margaret's lady stood nervously before her, wondering how to tell her that a young squire was waiting to see her. Margaret saw the woman was uncomfortable and asked about the matter. She received the news of the young squire with surprise.

"What does he want? Did you ask him?"

"Oh yes, but all he will say is he has a message for you, and he had sworn to place it in your hands only." Margaret was curious. "Bring him here so he can deliver his message." Her lady curtsied and hurried to bring the young squire to her.

Margaret watched as a very young boy entered the room. He was dressed elegantly in the latest fashion. Quite handsome, his blonde hair fell to his shoulder and curled beneath. Deep blue eyes looked directly into hers.

"What is your name?" she was fascinated by him. He gave a slight bow of his head. "John, my lady. John, son of Sir Thomas Edringham from York."

"You have a message for me, I understand, and will not leave it but must put it in my hands." She gave a slight laugh. "Well, who is this message from?"

He did not reply, simply withdrew it from under his cloak and handed it directly to her. She took it and immediately recognized Richard's seal. She paled. "Where did you get this from?" She turned the roll of parchment over in her hand.

"From King Richard." She looked up sharply. "He gave it to me before he died. May I go now?" He had kept his oath and delivered the letter. He didn't want to express how much he hated her and her son for what happened to the King he admired so much. She was looking at the letter again and hardly heard him, wondering why Richard had written this letter. John coughed to get her attention. He was glad she called a servant and told him to arrange refreshments for the young gentleman. Thanking him, she turned and sat in a chair by the window.

She broke the seal and unrolled the letter.

My dear Countess,

If you are reading this letter, I will have left this world, and your dreams will have been realized. Congratulations. But my interest in writing to you is of another matter. Very recently, in a most strange way, a letter came into my possession. A letter, my Lady, that was written for your eyes only. It was from the late William Collingbourne.

Oh yes. No doubt this information will add colour to your face, and by the sounds of things, it should. Whatever the secret and lies you have engaged in had the unfortunate result in William Collingbourne receiving the harshest form of punishment for a crime of which he apparently was not guilty. Your lies and scheming to get your son Henry on the throne apparently had no limits. Even those you supposedly loved suffered as a result.

It was my mistake not to have you executed for treason, of which you were found guilty. It was my mistake not to have put

Thomas, your husband, under lock and key instead of allowing him the freedom to retire for a short period from my services. I suspected he would betray me but hoped he would have enough decency to honor my trust. You know my philosophy, 'innocent until proven guilty'. Clearly, if you are reading this letter, it is too late to commiserate on my failings. My greatest disappointment is that I believed Collingbourne had betrayed me. I found out too late that your lies convinced the jury of his guilt. If your husband had read the letter, he was as guilty as you.

I should have known better. Collingbourne was a dear friend to Edward, my brother, all his life. He had proven his loyalty and friendship to me for many years when we worked on various commissions together. I have known him since when I was a boy.

I have pardoned him, although it is me who needs pardoning. I intend to reverse the attainment. I will give all his property back to his wife and children. But if you are reading this, my life has been taken from me before this pardon can be legally executed.

You owe him, Margaret. Your conscience should be troubling you at night. How do you sleep? He loved you so much that he accepted your blame to protect you.

You can do something about it. Ensure that your son, who no doubt is wearing my crown, will follow through and pardon Collingbourne. Encourage Henry to pardon him for your sins that enabled him to steal my crown. Give back to his wife and family that taken from them unjustly. It can be our secret.

You see, even from my grave, I seek justice.

Richard III

August 1485

Margaret put the letter away. She never wanted to read it again. For the first time, she was able to view what she had done without the obsession to get her son on the throne clouding her thoughts.

Her guilt was deep. She had loved Collingbourne but loved her son more. If she were honest, was it the idea of her son being king that drove her, not her love for him? She had not thought about the pain and suffering Collingbourne's family had to endure. She had not considered the way she had manipulated those who trusted her to achieve her goal. She wasn't sorry. Henry was king. The power was hers. Then with a sudden realisation, she recognised the truth. Power was what she sought. In putting Henry on the throne, she had put herself there. She knew she would continue to manipulate those who stood in her way. Elizabeth, Edward's daughter, would soon be queen, but she would never hold power over Henry. Elizabeth Woodville, the Dowager Queen, may have her status returned, but she would only have the power that suited the King's mother, not the Queen's.

Henry? Was not it a truism that 'it is the hand that rocks the cradle that rules the world'? He may believe he has the power, but she knew differently.

Collingbourne had understood her. He never sought power over her, but he knew she sought it for herself. Yet, he had been true to her, even at the cost of his own life.

Richard was right. She could do something about his pardon, and she would. Henry would want to reward those who gave him support, and Collingbourne would be one of them. Let him be pardoned, as Richard requested. He deserved it. Richard? Fortunately, dead men can't speak.

Afterword

While it is necessary to research the facts for a novel, it is sometimes impossible to get them. Many of the documents are incomplete or missing and it becomes extremely frustrating.

The *Titulus Regius* is the single most important contemporary document establishing Richard III's title to the crown of England. The grounds upon which Richard became king are clearly explained, and legally enshrined as an act of parliament. Henry VII later repealed the act unread and ordered the destruction of all copies. How fortunate that the original version, preserved in the rolls of parliament, remained untouched and we learn that Richard did not usurp the throne of England.

As far as Collingbourne is concerned, research revealed evidence of a commission of oyer and terminer, which included the Dukes of Suffolk, Norfolk, and the Earls of Surrey and Nottingham, the Viscounts Lovell and Lisle, three barons including

Lord High Constable Thomas Stanley and five justices of the King's Bench, including chief justice William Hussey.

We also have record of the date and place of the trial. It was held early in December at the Guildhall. Collingbourne was found guilty of high treason and sentenced to death. However, there is nothing available about the hearing. Why is this? Did Henry VII or even Margaret Countess of Richmond, have reason to destroy evidence?

Philllipa Langley's wonderful research that, against all odds, resulted in discovery of the body of Richard 500 years after his death demonstrates how wrong historians can be. Scientific research proved Richard was not the crippled, disfigured man Tudor propaganda had painted. Her findings support the view that the Richard III Society has promoted for years. Langley believed in King Richard, and somehow her sixth sense lead her to prove Richard's body was not previously exhumed and thrown into the nearby river soon after the Dissolution in 1538. What a wonderful story she unfolded. And there is more. Her next project, 'The missing Princes' is well underway.

Phillipa has proved if we look deeper, a more complex picture starts to appear. Richard is seen to be a law-maker whose driving force was a sense of fairness and justice.

An author can never really be sure of the truth. History provides a colourful background to any novel, but history is always, to some extent, a work of fiction. It is usually filtered through minds attitudes and conceptions of succeeding generations. In fact no one really knows what the truth is and this allows the author to speculate and invent, weaving the story as the imagination dictates.

Susan Collingbourne

About the Author

Susan is an Australian based author. A teacher of Literature and History for over thirty years, Susan holds a Master of Letters (Creative Writing) Bachelor of Arts, Diploma of Education, and a Professional Diploma of Children's Writing. Susan lives with her husband at the foothills of Strzelecki Ranges, West Gippsland, Victoria.

www.ingramcontent.com/pod-product-compliance
Lightning Source LLC
Chambersburg PA
CBHW041136110526
44590CB00027B/4034